J.C. RYLE ON PRAYER

31 INSIGHTS FOR UNDERSTANDING THE PURPOSE AND POWER OF PRAYER

GODLIPRESS TEAM

© Copyright 2022 by GodliPress. All rights reserved.

This book is copyright protected. You cannot amend, distribute, sell, use, quote or paraphrase any part, or the content within this book, without the consent of the author or publisher, except in the case of brief quotations embodied in critical articles or reviews.

Scripture quotations are from The ESV® Bible (The Holy Bible, English Standard Version®), copyright © 2001 by Crossway, a publishing ministry of Good News Publishers. Used by permission. All rights reserved.

CONTENTS

Introduction	vii
1. WATCH AND PRAY	1
The Flesh Is Weak	2
Daily Reflection	3
2. PRAYER—EVIDENCE OF THE SPIRIT	5
Daily Reflection	7
3. THE LORD'S PRAYER	9
Daily Reflection	12
4. A PRIEST WHO INTERCEDES FOR US	13
Daily Reflection	15
5. YOU MUST PRAY	17
Daily Reflection	20
6. STEADFAST, REGULAR PRAYER	21
Daily Reflection	23
7. REPENTANCE AND CONFESSION	25
Daily Reflection	28
8. INTIMATE PRAYER	29
Communion With Christ	29
Abiding in Christ	30
Daily Reflection	32
9. WHY PEOPLE DON'T PRAY	33
Daily Reflection	35
10. PERSEVERANCE IN PRAYER	37
Daily Reflection	39
11. FORGIVENESS IN PRAYER	41
Daily Reflection	43

12. THE HABIT OF PRAYER	44
Prayer Is Evidence	44
Teaching the Habit of Prayer	46
Daily Reflection	47

13. THE TAX COLLECTOR'S PRAYER	48
Pride of the Pharisee	48
Humility of the Tax Collector	49
Daily Reflection	51

14. ASK, SEEK, KNOCK	52
Daily Reflection	54

15. UNREAL PRAYING	56
Daily Reflection	59

16. THANKSGIVING	60
Mary's Prayer of Praise	61
Daily Reflection	63

17. DANIEL'S PERSONAL PRAYER LIFE	64
Daily Reflection	67

18. PROMISES IN PRAYER	68
Daily Reflection	71

19. THE DIFFERENCE IN CHRISTIANS	72
Daily Reflection	74

20. PRAYING IN THE POWER OF THE HOLY SPIRIT	76
Daily Reflection	78

21. EVERYTHING WE NEED TO PRAY	80
Daily Reflection	82

22. THE DANGER OF NEGLECTING PRIVATE PRAYER	83
Daily Reflection	86

23. THE BEST RECIPE FOR JOY	87
Jesus Takes Our Sorrows	89
Daily Reflection	90

24. PRAYER IS NECESSARY FOR GROWTH	92
Daily Reflection	94
25. JESUS PRAYS FOR HIS PEOPLE	96
To Sanctify Them	96
To Unite Them	97
To Be With Him	98
Daily Reflection	98
26. SALVATION AND PRAYER	100
Daily Reflection	102
27. PRAYER IS YOUR RESPONSIBILITY	103
No One Is Exempt	104
It Teaches Us	104
Daily Reflection	106
28. PRAYING FOR AN INCREASE OF FAITH	107
Do You Want More Faith?	108
Faith and Assurance	108
Daily Reflection	110
29. RUSHED PRAYERS	111
No Real Prayer	111
No Heart in Prayer	112
Poor Prayers Are Not Answered	113
Daily Reflection	114
30. ALERT, BOLD, AND SINCERE	115
Alert in Prayer	115
Bold in Prayer	116
Sincere in Prayer	117
Daily Reflection	118
31. MISSIONARY PRAYER	119
Daily Reflection	121
About J.C. Ryle	123
Bibliography	125

INTRODUCTION

J.C. Ryle's books, tracts, and sermons continue to be a source of inspiration and a challenge for many Christians across the globe in spite of the hundred years that have elapsed since he wrote and spoke these words.

It's not because he is the most descriptive writer or because he goes into deep biblical exegesis, verse by verse. It's because of his simple, direct approach. In fact, one of his most famous books, *Simplicity in Preaching*, is filled with hints and tips on how to bring the Gospel to people without trying to be clever or too eloquent. He was a very hands-on preacher, and this comes out clearly in all his messages, often adding applications to the ends of sermons for people to be able to apply what he said in practical ways to their own lives.

As we gathered chapters on the topic of prayer for this book, our aim was to present Ryle's best sermons and writings that will inspire and challenge you in this area of your Christian walk. We have merged some parts and had to shorten others to fit the format, but we have been very careful to preserve the spirit of what Ryle said and maintain his words. Though we've modernized the text, we have made sure that Ryle's meaning has not been lost and that you will receive the instructions as he intended.

The daily reflections are an addition to give you time to reflect and ponder over the chapter and to lead you into a deeper understanding of what you have just read. They are not meant to be methodically followed to the letter but are more of a guide to help you see areas you may need to focus on in your own life.

The aim is always to enhance our growth in prayer, as it is a vital link between us and God; without it, our relationship will suffer and fade.

1

WATCH AND PRAY

"Watch therefore, and pray always that you may be counted worthy to escape all these things that will come to pass, and to stand before the Son of Man"
Luke 21:36 NKJV

Let us learn from these verses about the special duties of Christians regarding Jesus' return. He sums them up in two words: watchfulness and prayer. "*Watch therefore,*" He says, "*and pray always.*"

We are to "*watch.*" We are to live on our guard like men in an enemy's country. We are to remember that evil is about us, near us, and in us—that we have to contend daily with a treacherous heart, an ensnaring world, and a busy devil!

Remembering this, we must put on the whole armor of God and beware of spiritual drowsiness. "*Let us not sleep, as others do,*" says Paul, "*but let us keep awake and be sober*" (1 Thess. 5:6).

We are to "*pray always.*" We are to keep up a constant habit of real, sincere prayer. We are to speak with God daily and hold daily communion with Him about our hearts. We are to pray especially for grace to lay aside every weight, and to cast away everything which may interfere with our readiness to meet our Lord. Above all, we are to watch our habits of devotion with godly jealousy and to beware of rushing over or shortening our prayers.

Let us act on this. If we believe that Christ is coming again—then let us get ready to meet Him. "*If you know these things, blessed are you if you do them*" (John 13:17).

The Flesh Is Weak

Let us also learn that there is great weakness, even in true disciples of Jesus, and that they need to watch and pray against it. We see Peter, James, and John—those three chosen apostles, sleeping when they should have been watching and praying. And we find Jesus addressing them in these serious words, "*Watch and pray that you may not enter into temptation. The spirit indeed is willing, but the flesh is weak*" (Matt. 26:41).

There is a double nature in all believers. Converted, renewed, sanctified as we are, we still carry about with us a mass of indwelling corruption, a body of sin. Paul speaks of this when he says, "*I find it to be a law that when I want to do right, evil lies close at hand. For I delight in the law of God, in my inner being, but I see in my members another law waging war against the law of my mind*" (Rom. 7:21-23). The experience of all true Christians of every age confirms this. They find inside them two contrary principles, and continual strife between the two. Jesus alludes to these two principles when He addresses His half-awakened disciples. He calls the one flesh and the other spirit. He says, "*The spirit indeed is willing, but the flesh is weak.*"

But does Jesus excuse this weakness of His disciples? No, He uses that very weakness as an argument for watchfulness and prayer. He teaches us that the very fact that we have this weakness should stir us up continually to "watch and pray."

If we desire to walk with God, and not fall like David or Peter, let us never forget to watch and pray. Let us live like men on the enemy's ground, and always be on our guard. We cannot walk too carefully. We cannot be too jealous of our souls. The world is very ensnaring. The devil is very busy. Let Jesus' words ring in our ears daily like a trumpet. Our spirits may sometimes be very willing. But our flesh is always very weak. Then let us always watch and always pray.

Daily Reflection

This chapter is a clear call for us not only to pray but to be alert and watch! Many of us simply fulfill our duty to pray without the slightest concern for anything else. And we also often find ourselves wanting to pray but not even getting that far! To be awake in our prayers is necessary if we want to be effective.

1. What do you understand 'watch' means?

2. Is it possible to "pray always"?
3. What is the dual nature Ryle speaks of? Read Romans 7:15-20.
4. How often do you find your flesh to be weak when it comes to prayer? What do you do about it?

2

PRAYER—EVIDENCE OF THE SPIRIT

"And he who searches hearts knows what is the mind of the Spirit, because the Spirit intercedes for the saints according to the will of God"
Romans 8:27

The effects that the Holy Spirit produces can always be seen. A person of the world may not understand them, but where the Spirit is, He will not be hidden. When He enters the heart, he does not lie still or sleep. He will make His presence known. He will shine out little by little through the windows of a person's daily habits and conversation and manifest to the world that He is in their life.

He is called, "*The Spirit of wisdom and of revelation*" (Eph. 1:17). It was the promise of Jesus that, "*he will teach you all things*" and "*he will guide you into all the truth*" (John 14:26; 16:13). We are all by nature ignorant of spiritual truth. "*The natural person does not accept the things of the Spirit of God, for they are folly to him*" (1 Cor. 2:14). Our eyes are blinded. We don't know God, Jesus, ourselves, the world, sin, heaven, or hell as we should. We see everything under false colors. The Spirit alters this state of things entirely. He opens the eyes of our understanding. He illumines us; He calls us out of darkness into marvelous light. He takes away the veil. He shines into our hearts, and makes us see things as they are!

The signs of the presence of the Holy Spirit in a person can be seen and discerned. Some of them stand out more clearly in some than in others—prayer is one of them. In my own experience, I never saw a truly godly person in whom these marks are not evident.

Can the person who never prays at all, or is content with saying a few formal, heartless words, have the Spirit?

He is called the Spirit "*of grace and pleas*" (Zech. 12:10). God's chosen are said to "*cry to him day and night*" (Luke 18:7). They cannot help it. Their prayers may be poor, weak, and wandering, but they must pray; something within them tells them they must speak with God and bring their needs before Him. Just as the baby will cry when it feels pain or hunger, because it is its nature, so the new nature implanted by the Holy Spirit will cause a person to pray. He has the Spirit of adoption, and he must cry, "*Abba! Father!*" (Gal. 4:6).

Where the Holy Spirit is, there will always be the habit of sincere personal prayer. He makes it as natural for a person to pray as it is for a baby to breathe; with this one difference

—the baby breathes without an effort, and the newborn soul prays with much conflict and strife. The person who knows nothing of real, living, passionate, personal prayer and is content with some old format, or with no prayer at all, is dead before God. They do not have the Spirit of Christ.

A man can preach from false motives. He can write books, make fine speeches, and seem diligent in good works, but still be a Judas Iscariot. But someone hardly ever goes into his room and pours out his soul before God in secret, unless they are sincere. God has put His stamp on prayer as the best proof of true conversion. When He sent Ananias to Saul in Damascus, He gave him no other evidence of his change of heart than this—"*Behold, he is praying*" (Acts 9:11).

I know that much can go on in a person's mind before they come to pray. They might have many convictions, desires, wishes, feelings, intentions, resolutions, hopes, and fears. But all these things are not very clear evidence. They can all be found in ungodly people as well, and often end in nothing. In many cases, they don't last longer than the morning mist or the dew that passes away. A real, sincere prayer, flowing from a broken and contrite spirit, is worth more than all these things put together.

Daily Reflection

Prayer may be private, from our hearts to God, performed in secret in our rooms, but the evidence of it is quite profound. Apart from a deeper personal relationship and awareness of Jesus in your life, there are signs that others can see. These are indications of the Spirit's active working in your life.

1. What is the role of the Holy Spirit?
2. What is your answer to this question: "Can the person who never prays at all, or is content with saying a few formal, heartless words, have the Spirit?"
3. Ryle lists some things that are *not* clear evidence of the Spirit in prayer. Do you sometimes have these?
4. Can you tell the difference between these and a "real, sincere prayer, flowing from a broken and contrite spirit"?

3

THE LORD'S PRAYER

*"Our Father in heaven, hallowed be your name.
Your kingdom come, your will be done, on earth as it is in heaven.
Give us this day our daily bread, and forgive us our debts,
as we also have forgiven our debtors.
And lead us not into temptation, but deliver us from evil"*
Matthew 6:9-13

The Lord's prayer has ten parts.

The first sentence declares who we pray to—"*Our Father in heaven.*" We cry to the everlasting Father, the Lord of heaven and earth. We are His children by faith in Jesus, and have "*the Spirit of adoption as sons, by whom we cry, 'Abba! Father!'*" (Rom. 8:15). This is the sonship we must desire if we would be saved. Without faith in Jesus' blood, and union with Him, it is useless to talk of trusting in the Fatherhood of God.

The second sentence is a petition about God's name—"*hallowed be your name.*" By the '*name*' of God, we mean all His attributes—His power, wisdom, holiness, justice, mercy, and truth. By asking that they be '*hallowed,*' we mean that they may be made known and glorified. The glory of God is the first thing that God's children should desire. It is the object of one of our Lord's own prayers—"*Father, glorify your name*" (John 12:28).

The third sentence concerns God's kingdom—"*Your kingdom come.*" This is the kingdom of grace that God sets up and maintains in the hearts of all Christians, by His Spirit and word. But we also mean the kingdom which will one day be set up, when Jesus will return.

The fourth sentence is a statement of God's will—"*your will be done, on earth as it is in heaven.*" We pray that God's laws may be obeyed by people as they are by angels in heaven. We ask that those who do not obey His laws may be taught to obey them and that those who do obey them may obey them better. This is perfect submission to God's will.

The fifth sentence is a request for our own daily needs—"*Give us this day our daily bread.*" We are taught to acknowledge our entire dependence on God for our daily necessities. We ask for '*bread*' as the simplest of our needs, and in that word, we include all that our bodies require.

The sixth sentence is a petition about our sins—"*forgive us our debts.*" We confess that we are sinners and need daily forgiveness. We condemn all self-righteousness and self-justification. We are instructed to continually confess at the throne of grace, and to continually seek mercy.

The seventh sentence professes our feelings toward others—we ask our Father to "*forgive us our debts, as we also have forgiven our debtors.*" This is the only profession in the whole prayer and the only part on which Jesus comments when He finishes the prayer. It is to remind us that we must not expect our prayers for forgiveness to be heard if we pray with hate in our hearts toward others. We must not expect to be forgiven if we cannot forgive.

The eighth sentence is a request about our weakness—"*lead us not into temptation.*" It teaches us that we can be led astray, and fall. It instructs us to confess our weakness and beg God to hold us up, and not allow us to run into sin. We ask Him to keep us from going into that which would injure our souls, and never to allow us to be tempted above what we are able to bear (1 Cor. 10:13).

The ninth sentence is a petition about our dangers—"*deliver us from evil.*" We are taught to ask God to deliver us from the evil in the world, in our own hearts, and the devil. We confess that we are constantly seeing, hearing, and feeling the presence of evil. And we ask Him, who alone can preserve us, to continually deliver from its power (John 17:15).

The last sentence is giving praise—"*Yours is the kingdom and the power and the glory forever*" (Matt. 6:13 NKJV). We declare that the kingdoms of this world belong to our Father—all '*power*' belongs to Him—and that He deserves all '*glory.*' We conclude by rejoicing that He is King of kings and Lord of lords.

May our hearts go together with our lips! Happy is the person who can call God their Father through Jesus, and can say a heartfelt '*Amen*' to all that the Lord's Prayer contains.

Daily Reflection

We all know the Lord's Prayer and have probably seen or heard it said, sung, or explained in many different ways. Ryle's approach is very straightforward and systematic. Breaking it up into ten parts, we can see that it is not a set of words that we need to memorize and repeat but a pattern that we can follow for our own heartfelt prayers.

1. What is your feeling when you hear or say the Lord's Prayer? Why?
2. Ryle says there are two meanings for the words "Your kingdom come." Why are they significant?
3. Why do you think Jesus focused on the profession in the seventh part of the prayer after he had taught it to His disciples?
4. The prayer begins and ends with giving glory to God. What does this teach us about prayer?

4

A PRIEST WHO INTERCEDES FOR US

"Since then we have a great high priest who has passed through the heavens, Jesus, the Son of God, let us hold fast our confession"
Hebrews 4:14

Christianity provides the very thing that our hearts and consciences require. The Bible reveals the Friend and Mediator that we need—Jesus. It tells us of the Priest that meets our needs—even Jesus, the Son of God. It shows Him as the Person that our longing hearts desire.

Jesus is carrying on the work of a Priest which He began on earth, in heaven. He took our nature on Him and became a man so that He might be perfectly fitted to be the Priest we require. As a Priest, He offered up His body and soul as a sacrifice for sin on the cross and made complete atonement for us with His blood. As a Priest, He ascended and passed through the veil and entered into the presence of God. As a Priest, He is now sitting on our behalf at the right hand of God; what He actively began on earth, He is actively carrying on in heaven.

True rest and inner peace will never come from anything but direct faith in Christ Himself and His finished work. Peace by confessing to a human priest, denying your body, attending church meetings, or receiving Communion as a ritual—is a delusion and a trap! It is only by coming straight to Jesus Himself, tired and heavily burdened, and by believing, trusting communion with Him, that our souls find rest. This is *"sincere and pure devotion to Christ"* (2 Cor. 11:3).

There is no other priest who can, in any way, be a mediator between yourself and God but Jesus. He said, *"No one comes to the Father except through me"* (John 14:6). No sinful child of Adam—whatever his role, standing, or title—can ever occupy Christ's place, or do what Christ alone is appointed to do. The priesthood is Christ's role, and it is one which He has never delegated to another. This is *"sincere and pure devotion to Christ."*

We must also be clear that this crucified Savior sits at the right hand of God, to make intercession for all who come to God by Him; that He represents and pleads for those who put their trust in Him; and that He has delegated His office of Priest and Mediator to no man. We need no one else. We do not need Virgin Mary, angels, saints, priests, or ordained or unordained people to stand between us and God—just the one Mediator, Christ Jesus.

Jesus is our Priest, always interceding for us in heaven. It is written, "*he is able to save to the uttermost those who draw near to God through him, since he always lives to make intercession for them*" (Heb. 7:25). Paul asks, "*Who is to condemn?*", and one reason he gives for why there is no condemnation for believers is the fact that "*Christ Jesus is the one who died—more than that, who was raised—who is at the right hand of God, who indeed is interceding for us*" (Rom. 8:34). We cannot be exactly sure how He does this, but we remember how He prayed for His people in John 17, and how He told Peter He prayed for him, that his faith might not fail (Luke 22:32). Our great High Priest knows how to intercede.

As our Priest, He presents the prayers of His people before God and obtains their hearing, acceptance, and favor. Like the Jewish Priest, He offers incense that is mingled with the prayers of His saints (Rev. 8:3). It is hard to understand how words of sinful creatures like us can ever come into the presence of God and do us any good. But in Jesus' hands, our petitions obtain a value that they do not have by themselves. Prayers that are worth nothing in themselves are powerful when offered through Christ, for the sake of Christ, through the mediation of Christ.

Daily Reflection

Jesus' role as a High Priest is often overlooked or not understood in its entirety, possibly because we try to draw a comparison with earthly priests. But His duties and capabilities go far beyond what any man could ever achieve. Jesus interceding for us is an integral part of our saving grace.

Coming to Jesus as a High Priest can completely transform the way we see our prayers.

1. Why can true rest not come through confessing to an earthly priest or pastor?
2. Why does Jesus have to intercede and plead for us?
3. Are the roles of Mediator and high priest the same in any way? Read 1 Timothy 2:5.
4. Have you ever prayed to Jesus as your High Priest?

5

YOU MUST PRAY

*"Seek the LORD while he may be found;
call upon him while he is near"*
Isaiah 55:6

Prayer is the life breath of a person's soul. Without it, we may have a name to live, and be counted as Christians—but we are dead in the sight of God. The feeling that we must cry to God for mercy and peace is a mark of grace; and the habit of spreading before Him our soul's needs is evidence that we have the spirit of adoption.

Prayer is the appointed way to obtain the relief of our spiritual necessities—it opens the storehouse of God, and sets the fountain flowing. If we do not have, it is because we do not ask.

Prayer is the way to receive the outpouring of the Spirit in our hearts. Jesus has promised the Holy Spirit, the Comforter to His people. He is ready to come down with all his precious gifts, renewing, sanctifying, purifying, strengthening, cheering, encouraging, enlightening, teaching, directing, and guiding into all truth. But He waits to be asked and begged.

But we fall so miserably short. Few pray—many go down on their knees, and say words, but few really pray. There are…

few who cry to God,

few who seek, as if they wanted to find,

few who knock, as if they hungered and thirsted,

few who wrestle with God,

few who strive with God sincerely for an answer,

few who give Him no rest,

few who continue in prayer,

few who watch in prayer,

few who always pray without ceasing, and do not get tired.

Yes! Few pray. It is just one of the things everyone assumes is done but is seldom practiced. It is everybody's duty, but hardly anybody does it.

If your soul is to be saved, you must pray. God has no dumb children! If you are to resist the world, the flesh, and the devil—you must pray. It is useless to look for strength in times of trial if you have not sought and asked for it before. You may be thrown together with those who never pray. You may have to sleep in the same room with someone who never asks anything of God. Still, you must pray.

I can believe you find difficulties with prayer—moments, times, and places. I don't have any rules to give on these. I leave them to your own conscience. You must be guided by circumstances.

Jesus prayed on a mountain;

Isaac prayed in the fields;

Hezekiah turned his face to the wall as he lay on his bed;

Daniel prayed by a river;

Peter, the Apostle, on the roof.

I have heard of young men praying in stables and haylofts. All that I ask is this—you must know what it is to "*go into your room*" (Matthew 6:6). There must be set times when you speak with God face to face—you must have your daily times for prayer. You must pray.

Prayer is the piece of spiritual armor that Paul names last in Ephesians 6—but in value and importance, it is first. This is your daily food if you are to travel safely through the wilderness of this life. It is only in the strength of prayer that you will get to the mountain of God.

A person who spends time on his knees uses their time well. Make time for this.

Think of David, king of all Israel—what does he say? "*Evening and morning and at noon I utter my complaint and moan, and he hears my voice*" (Psalm 55:17).

Think of Daniel. He had all the business of a kingdom on his hands, yet he prayed three times a day. See the secret of his safety while he was in wicked Babylon.

Think of Solomon. He begins his reign with prayer for help and assistance, and his wonderful prosperity.

Think of Nehemiah. He found time to pray to God, even when standing before King Artaxerxes. Think of the example these godly men have left you—and go and do the same.

Daily Reflection

It might sound a bit forward and abrupt, but Ryle gets straight to the point by giving us a clear mandate: Go and pray! If we are honest, we already know this. It's not a surprise to read this, but it might be a sober reminder or a challenging reprimand. But the bottom line is that as Christians, we must pray.

1. How do you rate your prayer life at this moment?
2. Read Romans 8:15. Why is prayer the evidence of the Spirit of adoption?
3. What guidelines does Ryle give for how, when, and where to pray? Why?
4. Of the four examples at the end, which do you most identify with in terms of prayer?

6

STEADFAST, REGULAR PRAYER

"Continue steadfastly in prayer, being watchful in it with thanksgiving
Colossians 4:2

Don't let any excuse make you give up prayer. Paul didn't say, "*Continue steadfastly in prayer*" and "*Pray without ceasing*" for nothing (Col. 4:2, 1 Thess. 5:17). He didn't mean people should always be on their knees, like the Euchitæ sect used to think. But he did mean that our prayers should be like the continual burnt offering—constantly persevered in every day—like seed-time and harvest, and summer and winter—a thing that should always happen at regular seasons—that it should be like the fire on the altar, not always consuming sacrifices, but never completely going out.

The person who desires to come out from the world and be separate must continuously and habitually make sure they are not swallowed up and absorbed in the things of the world.

True Christians will strive to do their duty in whatever position they are in, and do it well. Whether politicians, businessmen, bankers, lawyers, doctors, or farmers—they will try to do their work so that no one can find a reason to fault them. But they will not allow it to get between them and Jesus. If business is beginning to eat up their Sundays, Bible-reading, private prayer, and is bringing a cloud between them and Heaven, they will say, "Stop! There is a limit. I cannot sell my soul for position, fame, or gold!"

Like Daniel, they will make time for communion with God, whatever the cost may be. Like Havelock, they will deny themselves rather than lose time reading the Bible and saying prayers. In all this, they might stand alone. Many will laugh and tell them they don't need to be so strict. But they will resolutely hold the world at a distance, whatever the cost. They will choose prosperity in their hearts over being prosperous in this world. This requires immense self-denial, but this is a genuine biblical separation.

The true Christian will not waste their evenings away. Whatever others may do, they will always make time for quiet, calm Bible reading and prayer. The rule will prove a hard one to keep. It might make them seem antisocial and over-strict, but anything is better than rushed prayers, careless Bible reading, and a bad conscience. They might be in the minority and thought to be strange, but this is a genuine biblical separation.

Once you have begun the habit, never give it up. Your heart will sometimes say, "We have had family prayers; what's the harm of skipping private prayer?" Your body will sometimes say, "I am not well, or sleepy, or tired; I don't need to pray." Your mind will sometimes say, "I have important business to attend to; cut my prayers short." Look at these suggestions as coming directly from the devil. They are as good as saying, "Neglect your soul."

Never forget that you can link your morning and evening devotions with an endless chain of short prayers said throughout the day. Even in company, or business, or in the streets, you can be silently sending up little winged messengers to God, as Nehemiah did in the presence of King Artaxerxes (Neh. 2:4). And don't think that the time given to God is wasted. A Christian is never a loser in the long run by persevering in prayer.

Daily Reflection

Making a habit out of something can be good, as we are shaped by our daily routines. Instead of having mindless rituals that we simply follow out of necessity, Ryle is talking about making time for daily prayer because of its importance in sustaining us every day. It's not a once-off occurrence, but something we need to nurture and grow into if we want to properly realize this duty of prayer in our lives.

1. Do you have a set time for daily prayer?

2. Do you struggle to keep this session of prayer? Why?
3. What is the difference between habit and ritual?
4. Ryle talks about biblical separation. What do you understand by this phrase?
5. How often do your heart, body, and mind give excuses for skipping or rushing prayer? What do you usually do in these moments?

7

REPENTANCE AND CONFESSION

"If we confess our sins, he is faithful and just to forgive us our sins and to cleanse us from all unrighteousness"
1 John 1:9

All men and women are born in sin. "*All have sinned and fall short of the glory of God*" (Rom. 3:23). Before God, all are guilty. "*There is not a righteous man on earth who does good and never sins*" (Eccles. 7:20). Every child of Adam must confess sin.

Repentance is a complete change of our natural heart on the subject of sin. We are all born in sin. We naturally love sin. We take to sin as soon as we can act and think—just as a bird takes to flying, and a fish takes to swimming. No child needs school to learn deceitfulness, selfishness, passion, self-will, gluttony, pride, and foolishness. These are not picked up from bad friends or learned through lengthy teaching. They spring up by themselves. Now, when this heart of ours is changed by the Holy Spirit when this natural love of sin is cast out, then that change which the Bible calls 'repentance' takes place. The person in whom the change happens is said to 'repent.' He is called a repentant person.

He feels he must speak to God against whom he has sinned. Something within him tells him to cry, pray, and talk with God about the state of his own soul. He must pour out his heart and acknowledge his iniquities at the throne of grace. They are a heavy burden within him, and he can no longer keep silent. He will not hide anything. He goes before God saying, "I have sinned against You—my iniquity is great. God be merciful to me, a sinner!"

Jesus is the great High Priest. He is sealed and appointed by God the Father for that very purpose. It is His duty to receive and hear, and forgive sinners. It is written in the Bible that He is "*a high priest forever*" (Heb. 6:20). "*Since we have a great priest over the house of God, let us draw near with a true heart in full assurance of faith, with our hearts sprinkled clean from an evil conscience and our bodies washed with pure water*" (Heb. 10:21-22).

People are naturally asleep and must be woken up. We are blind and must be made to see. We are dead and must be made alive. If this was not the case, there would be no urgent need for confession. The Bible commands it. Reason agrees with it. Our conscience approves of it. And yet, the vast majority of us have no practical acquaintance with confession of sin. There is no heart that is in such a bad state that it does not feel sin.

Go today to the throne of grace, and speak to the great High Priest, the Lord Jesus Christ, about your soul. Pour out your heart before Him. Keep nothing back from Him. Acknowledge your iniquities to Him, and beg Him to cleanse them away. Say to Him, in David's words, *"For your name's sake, O Lord, pardon my guilt, for it is great"* (Psalm 25:11), and *"Hide your face from my sins, and blot out all my iniquities"* (Psalm 51:9). Cry to Him as the tax collector did in the parable: *"God, be merciful to me, a sinner!"* (Luke 18:13).

We will never stop being sinners as long as we are in our bodies. Every day we will find something to condemn in our thoughts, motives, words, or deeds. Every day we will find that we need the blood and the intercession of Christ. So, let us keep up daily prayers before the throne of grace. Let us daily confess our weaknesses at the feet of our merciful and faithful High Priest, and seek forgiveness. Let us daily hide under the shadow of His wings and cry, *"Nothing good dwells in me; You are a hiding place for me"* (Rom. 7:18, Psalm 32:7).

May we become more humble and yet more hopeful—more aware of our unworthiness and yet more ready to rejoice in Christ Jesus, and have no confidence in the flesh! May our prayers become more passionate, and our confessions of sin more real—our eyes more focused, and our walk with God much closer—our knowledge of Jesus more clear, and our love for Him much deeper—our citizenship in heaven more evident, and our separation from the world much clearer!

Daily Reflection

Don't rush these times of reflection. They can be very helpful in gaining a deeper understanding and seeing your state of heart and prayer before the Lord. This is a time of healthy and honest acknowledgment of where you are. Have your Bible close so that you can look up any related scriptures that are mentioned or come to your mind.

Repentance and confession can be very revealing and personal moments in our lives. Understanding this in prayer is important, as true confession and heartfelt repentance bring freedom to our Christian life.

1. What is repentance?
2. What is confession? Read 1 John 1:9.
3. Why is confession such an important part of repentance?
4. As a High Priest, Jesus intercedes for us. What is meant by the "intercession of Christ"?

8

INTIMATE PRAYER

"Abide in me, and I in you"
John 15:4

Communion With Christ

Communion with Christ is the privilege of those who are continually striving to grow in grace, faith, knowledge, and conformity to the mind of Jesus in all things—who forget what is behind, and do not consider themselves yet to have taken hold of it, but *"press on toward the goal for the prize of the upward call of God in Christ Jesus"* (Philippians 3:14). Union is the bud, but communion is the flower. Union is the baby, but communion is the strong man. He that has union with Christ does well, but he that enjoys communion with Him does far better. Both have one life, one hope, one heavenly seed in their hearts—one Lord, one Savior, one Holy Spirit, one eternal home: but union is not as good as communion!

The secret of communion with Jesus is to be continually living the life of faith in Him, and drawing out of Him every hour the supply that every hour requires. To me, said Paul, "*to live is Christ.*" I live, yet not I, but *"Christ who lives in me"* (Philippians 1:21; Galatians 2:20).

Communion like this is the secret of the abiding joy and peace in believing, which well-known Christians have possessed. They were humble, deeply convinced of their weaknesses and sin. They would have told you that Romans 7 described them. They understood every word of the 'Confession' we find in our prayer books. They would have always said, "Remembering our sins is painful; the burden of them is too much." But they were always looking to Jesus, and in Him, they were always able to rejoice. Communion like this is the secret to the amazing victories these men had over sin, the world, and the fear of death. They did not just sit, saying, "I leave it all to Jesus to do for me," but, strong in the Lord, they used the holy nature He had put in them, boldly and confidently, and were *"more than conquerors through him who loved"* them (Romans 8:37). Like Paul, they would have said, "*I can do all things through him who strengthens me*" (Philippians 4:13).

Abiding in Christ

By 'communion,' we mean the habit of "abiding in Christ" which Jesus speaks of, in John 15, as essential to Christian fruitfulness (John 15:4-8). Let it be understood that union with Christ is one thing, and communion is another. There can be no communion with the Lord Jesus without union first; but unfortunately, there can be union with Jesus, and little or no communion at all.

Jesus says, "*If you abide in me, and my words abide in you, ask whatever you wish, and it will be done for you*" (John 15:7). This is a specific promise of power and success in prayer. It all depends on whether we "abide in Christ" and His "words abide in us."

To abide in Jesus means to keep up a habit of constant close communion with Him—to always be leaning on Him, resting on Him, pouring out our hearts to Him, and using Him as our Fountain of life and strength, as our best Friend. To have His words abiding in us is to keep His sayings and commands continually in our minds, and to make them the guide of our actions, conduct, and behavior.

This kind of Christian will not pray in vain. Whatever they ask they will receive, so long as they ask according to God's mind. No work will be too hard, and no difficulty insurmountable. Asking, they will receive, and seeking, they will find. Well-known Christians like these were Martin Luther, the German Reformer, the martyr, Bishop Latimer, and John Knox, of whom Queen Mary said that she feared his prayers more than an army of twenty thousand men. "*The prayer of a righteous person has great power as it is working*" (James 5:16).

Now, why is there not much power of prayer like this in our own time? Simply because there is not much close communion with Jesus and very little strict conformity to His will. People do not "abide in Christ," and therefore, they pray in vain. Jesus' words do not abide in them, as their guide, and so their prayers do not seem to be heard. They ask and receive not because they ask wrong. This lesson must sink into our hearts. If we want answers to our prayers, we must carefully remember Jesus' directions. We must keep up intimate friendship with the great Advocate in heaven if our requests are to prosper.

Daily Reflection

Although this is designed so that a new chapter is read each day followed by the daily reflections, if you find that you need to reread a certain chapter and dwell a little longer to contemplate and understand it, then do so. Don't rush ahead simply to keep up with a predetermined goal of sticking to one chapter a day. Sometimes the Holy Spirit wants us to wait and be still so that He can reveal a deeper revelation of something in our hearts. Take your time, and allow Him to guide you.

1. Communion here does not refer to the breaking of bread. What does it mean in this context?
2. How does this relate to prayer?
3. What is the difference between union and communion?
4. Why is there no power in prayer these days?
5. Is there power in your prayers?

9

WHY PEOPLE DON'T PRAY

*"There is no one who calls upon your name,
who rouses himself to take hold of you"*
Isaiah 64:7

I thought that most Christians said their prayers, and many people prayed. But now, I have concluded that the most professing Christians do not pray at all.

It is not natural for people to pray. The carnal, human mind is in opposition to God. Man's heart desires to get far away from God and have nothing to do with Him. His feeling toward Him is not love but fear. Why should a man pray when he has no real sense of sin, no real feeling of spiritual need, no belief in unseen things, and no desire for holiness and heaven? Most men know and feel nothing about any of these things; they are walking in the broad way. It's very clear to me, so I will say it boldly: I believe that few people pray.

Do you not know that it's unfashionable to pray? It's just one of the things that many are ashamed to admit to doing. Hundreds would much rather head to the edge of a cliff or follow a lost hope than publicly confess that they pray every day. If forced to sleep in the same room as a stranger, many would go to bed without prayer rather than speak to God in front of the other person. To drive well, dress well, go out, be thought of as clever and agreeable—all this is fashionable, but not to pray. I can't state it enough. It's unbelievable that so many people are ashamed of a habit that is supposed to be common. I believe that few people pray.

Have you thought about the lives that many live? Is it realistic to imagine that people are praying against sin every day and night when we see them embracing sin? Is it possible that they pray against the world when they are entirely absorbed and caught up in its pursuits? Do we think they ask God for grace to serve Him when they don't show the slightest desire to serve Him at all? No! It's very obvious and clear that most people either ask nothing from God or don't mean what they say when they do ask—which is the same thing. Praying and sinning will never live together in the same heart. Prayer will consume sin, or sin will choke prayer. I can't let this go when I look at men's lives. I believe that few people pray.

Are you not aware of how many people are dying? When they are close to death, they are like strangers to God. Not only are they ignorant of His Gospel, but they have no power to speak to Him. Their efforts to reach God in those moments are painfully awkward, shy, and raw as if they are doing it for the first time. It's as if they need an introduction to God, and as if they had never talked with Him before. I remember hearing about a lady who was worried to have a pastor come and visit her when she was sick and dying. She wanted him to pray with her, and he asked what he could pray for, but she didn't know and couldn't tell him. She was unable to name one thing that he could ask God for her soul. All she wanted was the form of a minister's prayers. I can understand this; deathbeds reveal many secrets. I can't forget what I have seen of sick and dying people. This also leads me to believe that few people pray.

I cannot see your heart. I do not know your private history in spiritual things. But from what I see in the Bible and in the world, I know I can't ask you a more necessary question than the one I am asking now—do you pray?

Daily Reflection

It is sometimes helpful to write down notes as you read the chapter or work through questions. Recording verses, thoughts, or significant sentences will help to form a clearer path in your mind of what you are trying to understand. It is also a great way to keep track of any issues you may be dealing with and can revisit later.

1. Did you think the same as Ryle, that few Christians pray?

2. Why do you think this is?
3. "Praying and sinning will never live together in the same heart." What do you make of this statement?
4. How would you rate the prayer life in your church or your weekly groups?

10

PERSEVERANCE IN PRAYER

"That they ought always to pray and not lose heart"
Luke 18:1

The object of the parable of the widow is explained by Jesus to show his disciples that they should always pray and not give up. These words are closely connected with the second coming of Christ, which is spoken about in the previous chapter before this parable.

It is perseverance in prayer, during the long, weary intervals between the first and second comings, which Jesus is urging His disciples to keep up. We are in that interval, that in-between period ourselves. The subject, therefore, should interest us.

The parable teaches the great importance of perseverance in prayer. Jesus conveys this lesson by telling the story of a widow who has no friends, looking to find justice from a wicked judge—through sheer persistence. *"Though I neither fear God nor respect man,"* said the unjust judge, *"yet because this widow keeps bothering me, I will give her justice, so that she will not beat me down by her continual coming"* (Luke 18:4-5).

Jesus gives the application of the parable, *"And will not God give justice to his elect, who cry to him day and night? Will he delay long over them?"* (Luke 18:7). If persistence obtains so much from a wicked man, how much more will it obtain for the children of God—the Righteous Judge, their Father in Heaven!

The subject of prayer should always be interesting to Christians. Prayer is the very life breath of true Christianity. It is in prayer that true religion begins. It is in prayer that true religion flourishes. It is in prayer that it decays. Prayer is one of the first signs of conversion (Acts 9:11). Neglect of prayer is the road to a fall (Matt. 26:40-41). Whatever throws light on the subject of prayer is for our heart's health.

So, let it be deeply engraved in our minds, that it is far easier to begin a habit of prayer than it is to keep it up. The fear of death, prick of the conscience, or some excited feelings can make us begin praying. But to go on praying requires saving faith. We quickly become tired and give way to the suggestion of Satan, that "it is of no use." And then comes the time when the parable before us should be remembered. We must recall that Jesus told us *"always to pray and not lose heart."*

Do you ever feel a secret inclination to rush your prayers, shorten your prayers, become careless about your prayers, or leave your prayers out altogether? Let us be sure, when we do, that it is a direct temptation from the devil. He is trying to sap and undermine the very foundation of our hearts and lead us down to Hell.

Let us resist the temptation and throw it behind our backs. Let us decide to pray on steadily, patiently, perseveringly—let us never doubt that it is good for us. However long the answer may take, still let us pray on. Whatever sacrifice and self-denial it may cost us, still let us pray on. *"Pray without ceasing"* and *"Continue steadfastly in prayer"* (1 Thessalonians 5:17, Colossians 4:2). Let us arm our minds with this parable, and while we live, whatever else we make time for—let us make time for prayer.

Daily Reflection

Perseverance is one of the most talked-about aspects when it comes to prayer. Every book on prayer includes this as one of its chapters. Jesus even mentioned specific parables to explain their importance. There must be a good reason for this. Perhaps it is something that we struggle with or find difficult to maintain.

1. Read Luke 11:5-8. How does this parable relate to the one about the widow in Luke 18?
2. What is the difference between persevering and praying long?

3. What does "lose heart" mean to you?
4. Do you ever feel a secret inclination to rush your prayers, shorten your prayers, become careless about your prayers, or leave your prayers out altogether?

11

FORGIVENESS IN PRAYER

"And whenever you stand praying, forgive, if you have anything against anyone, so that your Father also who is in heaven may forgive you your trespasses"
Mark 11:25

Let us learn from these verses the necessity of a forgiving spirit toward others. This lesson is taught here in a striking way. There is no immediate connection between the importance of faith, of which Jesus spoke in the verses before this, and the subject of forgiving injuries in this verse. But the connecting link is prayer. First, we are told that faith is essential to the success of our prayers. But then it is added that no prayers can be heard which do not come from a forgiving heart.

The value of our prayers depends on the state of mind in which we offer them. But the point before us receives far less attention than it deserves. Our prayers must not only be sincere, passionate, and in the name of Jesus. They must contain one more ingredient. They must come from a forgiving heart. We have no right to look for mercy if we are not ready to extend mercy to others. We cannot feel the sinfulness of the sins we ask to have forgiven if we hold onto hatred toward other people. We must have the heart of a brother toward our neighbor on earth if we wish God to be our Father in heaven. We must not flatter ourselves that we have the Spirit of adoption if we cannot bear with others and refrain from hate.

This is a heart-searching subject. The amount of hatred, bitterness, and division among Christians is great. It is no wonder that so many prayers seem to be thrown away and unheard. It is a subject that should come to all Christians, whatever their status or class is. Everyone does not have equal gifts of knowledge and words in their approaches to God. But everyone can forgive their fellow men. It is a subject that Jesus has emphasized to impress on our minds. He has given it a prominent place in the Lord's prayer. We are all familiar with the words, *"forgive us our debts, as we also have forgiven our debtors"* (Matt. 6:12). It would be good if we think about what those words mean!

Let us do some serious self-inquiry. Do we know what it is to have a forgiving spirit? Can we forgive the injuries that we receive from time to time in this evil world? Can we pass over a transgression and pardon an offense? If not, where is our Christianity? If not, why should we wonder that our souls do not prosper? Let us resolve to amend our ways in this matter. Let us determine by God's grace to forgive, even as we hope to be forgiven. God's free forgiveness of sins is our highest privilege in this world. God's free forgiveness will be our only title to eternal life in the world to come. Then let us be forgiving during the few years that we are here upon earth.

Daily Reflection

Forgiveness is another subject we hear about so often and agree with but struggle to apply in our own lives. Probably because it requires so much of us. But we often forget that although it is an action of the heart, it is also an act of prayer. Bringing a person or event before the Lord and asking forgiveness requires us to confess and ask, which is prayer!

1. Do you find it easy to forgive others?
2. Do you agree with this statement: "No prayers can be heard which do not come from a forgiving heart"?
3. Read the parable in Matthew 18:21-35. What is your understanding of forgiveness in this story?
4. Do you know someone you struggle to forgive, even though you have tried already? Have you asked the Lord to give you more of a forgiving spirit?

12

THE HABIT OF PRAYER

"Behold, he is praying"
Acts 9:11

Prayer Is Evidence

Prayer is one of the first signs that someone is born again. When God sent Ananias to Saul, he said, *"Behold, he is praying."* He had begun to pray, and that was proof enough.

Prayer was the distinguishing mark of the separation between God's people and the world. *"People began to call upon the name of the LORD"* (Gen. 4:26).

Prayer is the distinguishing trait of all real Christians now. They pray—for they tell God their needs, their feelings, their desires, their fears; and mean what they say. A so-called

Christian may repeat prayers, and good prayers too, but goes no further.

Prayer is the turning point in a person's soul. Our ministry is unprofitable, and our labor is vain until we are brought to our knees.

Prayer is one great secret of spiritual prosperity. When there is personal communion with God, your soul will grow like the grass after rain. When there is little prayer, everything will be at a standstill, you will hardly keep your soul alive. Show me a growing Christian, a strong Christian, a flourishing Christian, and you will find one that speaks often with the Lord. They ask much and have much. They tell Jesus everything, and so always know how to act.

Prayer is the mightiest resource God has placed in our hands. It is the best weapon to use in every difficulty and a cure for every trouble. It is the key that unlocks the treasury of promises, and the hand that grabs hold of grace and help in time of need. It is the cry He has promised to always listen to and answer, as a loving mother to the voice of her child.

Prayer is the simplest means for us to use in coming to God. It is within all of our reach—the sick, the aged, the infirm, the paralytic, the blind, the poor, the uneducated—all can pray. You cannot blame lack of memory, lack of learning, lack of books, and lack of education on this matter. As long as you have a tongue to tell your heart's state, you can and must pray. *"You do not have, because you do not ask"* (James 4:2), will be a terrible condemnation for many on the day of judgment.

Teaching the Habit of Prayer

Parents, if you love your children, do all that lies in your power to train them up in a habit of prayer. Show them how to begin. Tell them what to say. Encourage them to persevere. Remind them if they become careless and lazy about it. Do not let it be your fault if they never call on the name of the Lord.

This is the first step in Christianity that a child can take. Long before they can read, you can teach them to kneel by your side and repeat the simple words of prayer and praise. And, as the first steps are always the most important, so is the way your children's prayers are prayed. Watch that they don't say them quickly, carelessly, and irreverently. This is not a job for others to teach your kids or to teach themselves. If you never hear your children pray yourself, you are to blame.

Prayer is a habit that we remember the longest. Many old people could tell you how their mother used to make them pray when they were children. Other things, like the church they went to, the pastor who preached, the friends who used to play with them—all might be forgotten. But you will often find it is different with their first prayers. They will often be able to tell you where they knelt and what they were taught to say. It will be clear in their mind as if it was yesterday.

Reader, if you love your children, I urge you not to let the seed-time of a prayerful habit disappear without being planted. If you train your children in anything, train them in a habit of prayer.

Daily Reflection

Habits are good for us, especially if they are good habits! Learning to do good things continually is always beneficial. With prayer, we need to cultivate it into a habit, but not just a daily duty; a lively, active encounter of our hearts and souls with God. Learning it when we are young is the best, but like any habit, it can be learned no matter our age or occupation.

1. Look at all the things Ryle lists that prayer is. Which one do you identify with the most? Why?
2. Why do you think prayer is the first step for a child to take in Christianity?
3. What do you think it is about people praying that we remember the most?
4. Read Proverbs 22:6. What do you understand by this verse?

13

THE TAX COLLECTOR'S PRAYER

"God, be merciful to me, a sinner!"
Luke 18:13

Luke tells us clearly that "*He also told this parable to some who trusted in themselves that they were righteous, and treated others with contempt*" (Luke 18:9).

Pride of the Pharisee

We are all naturally self-righteous. It is the family disease of all the children of Adam. From the highest to the lowest—we think more highly of ourselves than we should. We secretly flatter ourselves, that we are not as bad as some, and that we have something to gain favor with God.

We read the prayer of the Pharisee, which Jesus condemns: *"God, I thank you that I am not like other men, extortioners, unjust, adulterers, or even like this tax collector. I fast twice a week; I give tithes of all that I get"* (Luke 18:11-12).

One great defect stands out in this prayer—it shows no sense of sin or need—no confession or petition—no acknowledgment of guilt or emptiness—no supplication for mercy and grace. It is just boasting. It is a proud, high-minded profession, without repentance, humility, and love. It hardly deserves to be called prayer at all.

No state of the heart can be as dangerous as that of the Pharisee. People's hearts are in a hopeless condition when they are not aware of their sins. In all our self-examination, let us not test ourselves by comparisons with other people. Let us look at nothing but the requirements of God. He who acts on this principle will never be a Pharisee.

Humility of the Tax Collector

Then we see the prayer of the tax collector, which Jesus commends. His prayer was the opposite of the Pharisee's. He stood far away, beating his chest, and said: *"God, be merciful to me, a sinner!"* (Luke 18:13). Jesus says, *"I tell you, this man went down to his house justified, rather than the other"* (Luke 18:14).

There are five points we notice in the tax collector's prayer.

1. It was a real petition. A prayer that only contains thanksgiving and profession, and asks nothing is

essentially defective. It may be suitable for an angel, but it is not suitable for a sinner.

2. It was a personal prayer. He did not speak of his neighbors—but himself. Vagueness and generality are defects of most people's faith. To get out of "we," "our," and "us" into "I," "my," and "me" is a great step toward Heaven.

3. It was a humble prayer, a prayer that put self in the right place. The tax collector confessed plainly that he was a sinner. This is the very starting point of saving Christianity. We never begin to be good until we can feel and confess that we are bad.

4. It was a prayer in which mercy was the main thing desired. Mercy is the first thing we must ask for when we begin to pray. Mercy and grace must be the subject of our daily petitions at the throne of grace, until the day we die.

5. Finally, the tax collector's prayer was from his heart. He was deeply moved by saying it. He beat his chest, like someone who felt more than he could express. Such prayers are the prayers that are God's delight. A broken and a contrite heart, He will not despise (Psalm 51:17).

Then Jesus says, "*Everyone who exalts himself will be humbled, but the one who humbles himself will be exalted*" (Luke 18:14).

The principle here is so frequently found in the Bible that it ought to be deeply engraved in our minds. Humility was a leading character in Abraham, Jacob, Moses, David, Job, Isaiah, and Daniel. It should be a leading character in all who profess to serve Christ. Not everyone has money to give. Not everyone is called to preach, write, or fill a prominent place in the church. But everyone is called to be humble.

Daily Reflection

This is one of Jesus' most famous examples of how to and how not to pray. It was so vivid and clear that it needs no explanation. Unfortunately, we all wish we were more like the tax collector and a lot less like ourselves—Pharisees that pray. When we are aware of the importance of humility in our prayer, we quickly become aware of how much pride we often bring with us when we pray.

1. Do your prayers tend to be more like the Pharisee or the tax collector? Why?
2. What was the Pharisee's great failure in his prayer?
3. Do you find it easy to be humble in prayer?
4. Why do you think humility in our prayers is so important to God?

14

ASK, SEEK, KNOCK

"Ask, and it will be given to you;
seek, and you will find;
knock, and it will be opened to you"
Matthew 7:7

Jesus uses three different words to express the idea of prayer. "Ask." "Seek." "Knock." He gives the widest, fullest promise to those who pray. "*Everyone who asks receives*" (Matt. 7:8).

Few of His sayings are so well known and so often repeated as this. The poorest and most uneducated can tell you that "if we do not seek—then we shall not find." But what is the good of knowing it if we do not use it? Do we know anything of this asking, seeking, and knocking?

There is nothing as simple and plain as praying—if someone has a desire to pray. Sadly, there is nothing that we are so slow to do as sincere, personal prayer. We will use many forms of religion, attend many meetings, and do many right things before we will do this. And yet without this, no soul can be saved.

Do we pray? Then let us carry on and not faint. It is not useless. It will bear fruit after many days. That promise has never yet failed, "*Everyone who asks receives.*"

"*Ask, and it will be given to you; seek, and you will find; knock, and it will be opened to you.*" The solemn declaration which follows appears intended to convince us even more: "*For everyone who asks receives, and the one who seeks finds, and to the one who knocks it will be opened*" (Matt. 7:8). The argument which concludes the passage leaves faithlessness and unbelief without excuse: "*If you then, who are evil, know how to give good gifts to your children, how much more will your Father who is in heaven give good things to those who ask him!*" (Matt. 7:11).

These same last words in Luke's version deserve special notice. The Holy Spirit is beyond doubt the greatest gift that God can give us. Having this gift, we have all things—life, truth, hope, and Heaven. Having this gift, we have God the Father's boundless love, God the Son's atoning blood, and full communion with all three Persons of the blessed Trinity. Having this gift, we have grace and peace in the present world—and glory and honor in the world to come. And yet this mighty gift is held out by Jesus, as a gift to be obtained by prayer! "*The heavenly Father give the Holy Spirit to those who ask him!*" (Luke 11:13).

Few passages in the Bible completely strip us of our excuses, as this passage. We are weak and helpless, but do we ask to be made strong? We are wicked and corrupt, but do we seek to be made better? We can do nothing of ourselves, but do we knock at the door of mercy and pray for the grace of the Holy Spirit? We are what we are because we have no real desire to be changed. We have not, because we ask not.

Do we know anything of real prayer? Do we pray at all? Do we pray in the name of Jesus, and as needy sinners? Do we know what it is to "ask," "seek," "knock," and wrestle in prayer?

If we do pray, then let it be a rule with us never to give up the habit of praying, and never to shorten our prayers. Our state before God can always be measured by our prayers. Whenever we begin to feel careless about our personal prayers, we can be sure there is something very wrong with the condition of our souls.

Daily Reflection

A book on prayer would not be complete without the obligatory "Ask, seek, knock." The most famous three words when it comes to the kingdom of God. And yet, we struggle to understand the very basics of this simple statement. Ryle, however, doesn't labor on these too much but looks at the important connection between them and the verses that follow which opens our understanding a little more to the heart behind Jesus' words.

1. Which one are you best at doing in prayer: asking, seeking, or knocking?
2. Why do you think we are quick to fulfill other religious duties but slow to pray?
3. What is the impact of Matthew 7:11 when attached to asking, seeking, and knocking?
4. What excuses do you sometimes give for not praying, or not praying as you should?

15

UNREAL PRAYING

*"These people draw near to Me with their mouth,
and honor Me with their lips,
but their heart is far from Me"*
Matthew 15:8 (NKJV)

Is there such a thing as unreal praying? There is. Jesus condemns it as one of the special sins of the Pharisees that *"for a pretense make long prayers"* (Mark 12:40). He does not charge them with not praying, or with praying too short. Their sin lay in that their prayers were not real.

Is there such a thing as unreal worship? There is. Jesus says of the Jews: "*These people draw near to Me with their mouth, And honor Me with their lips, But their heart is far from Me.*" They had plenty of formal services in their temples and synagogues, but the fatal defect was a lack of reality and lack of heart.

Paul tells us that we may "*speak in the tongues of men and of angels,*" and yet be no better than "*a noisy gong or a clanging cymbal*" (1 Cor. 13:1).

These verses show the importance the Bible attaches to reality in Christianity—that we need to watch, otherwise our belief becomes nominal, formal, unreal, and base. There has never been a time since the church began when there has not been a huge unreality and nominal religion among professing Christians. It is the same today.

Wherever I look, I see reasons for the warning, "Beware of unreality in religion. Be genuine. Be thorough. Be real. Be true."

Nothing is so dangerous to a person's soul. Familiarity with the form of religion, while we neglect its reality, has a deadening effect on the conscience. It grows a thick crust of insensibility over our hearts. None seem to become so desperately hard as those who are continually repeating holy words and handling holy things, while their hearts are running after sin and the world. People who have family prayers formally, to keep up a good appearance in their households; ministers who are reading prayers and Bible lessons every week in which they feel no real interest; people who are constantly reading responses and saying "Amen" without feeling what they say; singers, who sing the most spiritual songs every Sunday, only because they have good voices, while their hearts are entirely on other things. They are gradually hardening their hearts and searing the skin of their consciences. If you love your soul, beware of formality!

Do you think God does not see the heartlessness and deadness of our Christianity? Though we might deceive neighbors, friends, fellow worshipers, and ministers with a form of godliness, do we think that we can deceive God? He who formed the eye—won't He see? He knows the secrets of the heart. He will judge the secrets of men on the last day. He who said to each angel of the seven churches, "*I know your works*" (Rev. 2:19), is not changed. He who said to the man without the wedding clothes, "*Friend, how did you get in here?*" (Matt. 22:12) will not be deceived by a little cloak of outward religion.

Your religion, if it is real, and given by the Holy Spirit, must be in your **heart**. It must hold the reins. It must sway the emotions. It must lead the will. It must influence the choices and decisions. It must fill the deepest, lowest, inmost seat in your soul.

A right heart is a **praying** heart. It has in it "*Spirit of adoption as sons, by whom we cry, 'Abba! Father!'*" (Rom. 8:15). Its daily feeling is, "*Your face, LORD, do I seek*" (Psalm 27:8). It is drawn by a habitual need to speak to God about spiritual things—weak, and imperfect—but speak it must. It finds it necessary to pour out itself before God, as before a friend, and to spread before Him all its needs and desires. It tells Him all its secrets. It keeps back nothing from Him. You might as well try to persuade a man to live without breathing, as to persuade the owner of a right heart to live without praying.

Daily Reflection

No one wants to be accused of being unreal or false in their actions and motives, and yet many of us end up being just that. With prayer it seems to come easier to us to pretend—our mouths speak but our hearts are far away! But God is always searching our hearts, and there is no hiding the truth of what we are doing before Him.

1. Can you think of times you have been unreal in your prayers? Why did it happen?
2. Read Jeremiah 17:10. What is the meaning of this in relation to this chapter?
3. What is the importance of the Holy Spirit in connection with our prayers being real?
4. Which one do you think is mostly a "right heart": praying, worshiping, Bible reading, or preaching?

16

THANKSGIVING

"Give thanks in all circumstances; for this is the will of God in Christ Jesus for you"
1 Thess. 5:18

Unfortunately, there is too much complaining and too little thanksgiving among Christians! There is too much grumbling, and wanting things that we do not have. There is too little praise for the many blessings we have.

Murmurings, complaints, and discontent are all around us. Many hide their blessings under a bush and place their needs and hardships on a hill. This should not be the way, but all who know the ways of mankind, admit that it is true. The widespread thanklessness of Christians is a disgrace. It is proof of our lack of humility.

Thankfulness is a rare thing. We are told that of all the ten lepers whom Christ healed, there was only one who turned back and gave Him thanks. Jesus' words on this occasion are sobering, *"Were not ten cleansed? Where are the nine?"* (Luke 17:17).

This lesson is humbling, heart-searching, and very instructive. The best of us are far too much like the nine lepers. We are more ready to pray than to praise; and quick to ask God for what we do not have, but slow to thank Him for what we have.

Make every effort to be more thankful. Pray that you may know more and more what it is to *"rejoice in the Lord"* (Phil. 3:1). Learn to have a deeper sense of your sinfulness, and to be very grateful that by the grace of God, you are what you are. Is your heart right? Then be thankful. Praise the Lord for His mercy in calling *"you out of darkness into his marvelous light"* (1 Pet. 2:9).

Think about what you were by nature. Think about what has been done for you through free, undeserved grace. Your heart may not be all that it should be, or what you hope it will be, but it is not the old hard heart that you were born with. The person whose heart is changed should be full of praise.

Mary's Prayer of Praise

Look at the passionate thankfulness of Mary. It stands out clearly in all the beginning of her song.

- Her *"soul magnifies the Lord"* (Luke 1:46).

- Her "*spirit rejoices in God*" (Luke 1:47).
- "*All generations will call me blessed*" (Luke 1:48).
- "*Has done great things for me*" (Luke 1:49).

It is good to follow Mary's example and cultivate a thankful spirit. Let us wake up every morning with a deep conviction that we are debtors, and that every day we have more blessings than we deserve. Let us look around every week, as we travel through the world, and see if we do not have much to thank God for. It is good if our prayers and supplications had more thanksgiving in them (Phil. 4:6).

Let us pray every day for a thankful spirit that God loves and delights to honor. David and Paul were thankful men. It is the spirit that has marked all the godly men through the ages. It is the spirit that is the very atmosphere of Heaven. It is the spirit that is the source of life on earth. If we do not want to be anxious, then we must make our requests known to God—not only with prayer and supplication but with thanksgiving.

Above all, let us pray for a deeper sense of our sinfulness, guilt, and undeserving. This is the true secret of a thankful spirit. This is the person who always feels indebted to grace and always remembers that he deserves nothing but Hell— this is the person who will always be thanking and praising God. Thankfulness is a flower that will never bloom well— except on a root of humility!

Daily Reflection

Discussing these reflections with others can be very helpful. Working through them in a group or talking about what you have learned with someone you trust can open up your mind even more and bring another aspect to your understanding. Be encouraged, and even challenged, in your honesty and vulnerability with other people. It is a time of growth.

1. Do you find it easier to complain or to give thanks?
2. Why do you think Ryle says "Thankfulness is a rare thing"?
3. Why do you think having a "deeper sense of our sinfulness, guilt, and undeserving" is important to be thankful?
4. What is the connection between humility and thanksgiving?

17

DANIEL'S PERSONAL PRAYER LIFE

"He got down on his knees three times a day and prayed and gave thanks before his God, as he had done previously"
Daniel 6:10

It would be difficult to find a better testimony of a man's character than in these words: "*We shall not find any ground for complaint against this Daniel unless we find it in connection with the law of his God*" (Daniel 6:5). The world is always to find fault with Christians—how closely our conduct is watched, how eagerly our failings are proclaimed—and happy are those who by grace can live, that unbelievers can find no complaint against them.

Daniel's habit of private prayer was the hidden cause of all his steadiness, and it was accidentally discovered on this occasion. His enemies had obtained a decree from the king, that whoever should ask anything of any God for thirty days should be thrown into the den of lions. And having laid this trap for this holy man, we read that they found Daniel praying to God.

He was in the habit of kneeling and praying three times a day; this was also the practice of David, as we read in the Psalms, and this was the spirit of the centurion in the Acts, who always prayed to God. So, Paul encourages the Ephesians to pray always with all prayer and supplications, and the Thessalonians to pray without ceasing (Eph. 6:18, 1 Thess. 5:17). It has also been the habit of all the most prominent Christians: They were not content with a few cold, heartless words every morning and every night, they lived in the spirit of prayer and sent up many short, sincere requests throughout the day.

We are told that Daniel often prayed with his windows open toward Jerusalem. He did this, and so did every righteous Jew, not only because it was the land of his fathers and the land of promise, not simply because God would be worshiped there and there only—but mainly because all the emblems of the Messiah, the one way of salvation, the altar, the sacrifice, and the high priest were to be found there. And so also we, if we would have our prayers heard, must pray toward Jesus, the true Temple, our Altar, our High Priest, and our Sacrifice. These are the prayers that God will answer; this is the only way by which we can draw near with confidence and find grace to help in time of need. Understand the habit of private prayer: It is the secret of that steadiness that

Daniel showed in Babylon. It kept him upright in the middle of temptations.

We know that he had all the concerns of the government on his shoulders; he must have been surrounded by the business and affairs of nations—but none of these things prevented him from drawing near to God. People say, "We cannot do the things you ask us to do; we cannot come to Jesus on these terms. There would be no living in the world, no caring for our families, if we took your advice. We have no time for such Christianity; we cannot all give up the world." Look at holy Daniel! He had the responsibility of millions on his hands, he was the chief among the presidents of an empire, he had the management of kingdoms and their affairs; and yet he found time to be a faithful servant of God. He found time to cultivate the vineyard of his soul and walked with God as few have ever walked.

He was also not someone to say, "I am a chosen servant of God, I need not be so anxious about my needs"; he knew that God would keep him, but not unless he prayed to have protection, with diligence in grace. Many people who think they will find blessings and mercy while they neglect regular, heartfelt private devotion will be judged by this benchmark!

Is there anyone who is a humble follower of Jesus among you? Put Daniel before you. Be bold, be faithful, be humble, be persevering; endeavor to walk so uprightly that all may glorify God on your behalf, that no one can find a complaint against you except the way you follow the law of your God.

Daily Reflection

Daniel's prayer life stands out in the Bible simply because it was exposed as the main part of his enemies' scheming plot to bring him down. They could find nothing else but what he was doing right to accuse him of. Thankfully, in hindsight, we have the full picture and can appreciate his steadfast commitment to prayer, and admire him because of it.

1. What is the significance of adding the words *"as he had done previously"* in the verse?
2. Ryle uses the word 'steadiness.' What is the connection with prayer?
3. Do you have a habit of prayer? Describe it.
4. Would anyone be able to find a complaint against you concerning your prayers?

18

PROMISES IN PRAYER

"He has granted to us his precious and very great promises, so that through them you may become partakers of the divine nature"
2 Peter 1:4

There are incredible and precious promises to those of us who pray. What did Jesus mean when He said these words?

- *"Ask, and it will be given to you; seek, and you will find; knock, and it will be opened to you. For everyone who asks receives, and the one who seeks finds, and to the one who knocks it will be opened"* (Matt. 7:7-8).
- *"And whatever you ask in prayer, you will receive, if you have faith"* (Matt 21:22).

- *"Whatever you ask in my name, this I will do, that the Father may be glorified in the Son. If you ask me anything in my name, I will do it"* (John 14:13-14).
- What did He mean in the parables of the friend at midnight and the persistent widow? (Luke 11:5 and 18:1).

Think about these verses. If these are not an encouragement to pray, then the words have no meaning at all.

There are wonderful examples in the Bible of the power of prayer. Nothing seems to be too great, too hard, or too difficult for prayer to do. It has achieved things that seemed impossible and out of reach. It has won victories over fire, air, earth, and water. Prayer opened the Red Sea. Prayer brought water from the rock and bread from heaven. Prayer made the sun stand still. Prayer brought down fire from the sky on Elijah's sacrifice. Prayer turned the counsel of Ahithophel into foolishness. Prayer overthrew the army of Sennacherib.

No wonder Mary, Queen of Scots, said, "I fear John Knox's prayers more than an army of ten thousand men."

Prayer has healed the sick. Prayer has raised the dead. Prayer has brought about the conversion of souls. "The child of many prayers," a Christian once said to Augustine's mother, "shall never perish." Prayer, suffering, and faith can do anything. Nothing seems impossible when a man has the spirit of adoption. *"Let me alone"* (Exodus 32:10), are the remarkable words of God to Moses, when Moses was about to intercede for the children of Israel. The Chaldee translation is, "leave off praying." As long as Abraham asked mercy for Sodom, the Lord went on giving. He never stopped giving it until Abraham stopped praying. When you think about this, isn't this an encouragement?

What more can a person want to guide them to grow spiritually than the things I have just told you about prayer? What more can be done to make the path to the mercy seat easier, and to remove all obstacles from the sinner's way? If the demons in hell had a door like this opened before them, they would jump for joy and scream with happiness.

But where will the person who neglects such amazing encouragement hide their head? What can be said for the person who dies without prayer after all of this? I hope that you are not that person.

Let us learn to rest on promises and embrace them as Zachariah did. We must not doubt that every word of God about His people's future will be fulfilled. Their safety is secured by promise. The world, the flesh, and the devil shall never succeed against any believer. Their deliverance on the last day is secured by promise. They will not come under condemnation but be presented spotless before the Father's throne. Their final glory is secured by promise. Their Savior shall come again to gather us together and to give us a crown of righteousness. Let us be persuaded of these promises. Let us embrace them and not let them go. They will never fail us. God's word is never broken. He is not a man that He should lie. We have a seal on every promise which Zachariah never saw. We have the seal of Jesus' blood to assure us that what God has promised, God will perform.

Daily Reflection

Promises in prayer are vital. Without them, we would have very little to base our requests and faith on to receive answers. Many writers, like Spurgeon, encourage us to use these as arguments or leverage when bringing our petitions to God. If anything, promises should be encouraging to us.

1. Have you ever prayed to God holding one of His promises up as a guarantee to receive what you were asking for?
2. Does it seem presumptuous or arrogant to you to do this?
3. Doubt and promises seldom work together. Do you doubt God's promises?
4. Read Hebrews 10:23. Explain it.

19

THE DIFFERENCE IN CHRISTIANS

"As he who called you is holy, you also be holy in all your conduct"
1 Peter 1:15

We are all fighting the same good fight, but some fight more courageously than others! We are all doing the Lord's work, but some do much more than others! We are all light in the Lord, but some shine brighter than others! We are all running the same race, but some go faster than others! We all love the same Lord and Savior, but some love Him more than others!

What is the reason that some believers are so much brighter and holier than others? I believe the difference in nineteen out of twenty cases comes from different habits in personal prayer. I believe that those who are not very holy, hardly pray, and those who are very holy, pray a lot.

I am sure this opinion will surprise some people. I have little doubt that many see great holiness as a special kind of gift, which only a few pretend to aim at. They admire it from a distance in books. They think it's beautiful when they see an example near them. But other than something that's within reach of only a very few, such a notion never seems to enter their minds. In short, they consider it a kind of monopoly granted to a few favored believers, but certainly not to everyone.

Now, I believe that this is a very dangerous mistake. I believe that spiritual, as well as natural, greatness depends far more on what is within everyone's reach than on anything else. Of course, I don't say we have a right to expect a miraculous handout of intellectual gifts. But I will say that when a person is born again, whether they are very holy or not, depends mainly on his diligence in using God's appointed methods. And I can confidently add that the principal way that most believers have become great in the church is through the habit of diligent and private prayer.

Look at the lives of the brightest and best of God's servants, whether they were in the Bible or not. See what is written about Moses, David, Daniel, and Paul. Notice what is recorded about Luther and Bradford, the Reformers. Observe what is told of the private devotions of Whitefield, Cecil, Venn, Bickersteth, and M'Cheyne. Tell me about any of these saints and martyrs that did not have this obvious, prominent sign—they were men of prayer. You can depend on this, prayer is power!

Prayer brings a fresh and continued outpouring of the Spirit. He alone begins the work of grace in a person's heart. He alone can carry it forward and make it prosper. But the Spirit loves to be begged, and those who ask the most will always receive the most of His influence.

Prayer is the most definite cure against the devil and nagging sins. Any sin that is properly prayed against will never stand strong. The devil will never hold dominion over us in any area that we ask the Lord to deal with. But, we must state our case to our heavenly Doctor, so He can give us daily relief. We must drag those demons that are pestering us to Jesus' feet, and cry to Him to send them back to hell.

Do you wish to grow in grace and be a very holy Christian? Then Pray.

Daily Reflection

This is not a surprise to us, to read that there are different degrees of Christians. But it is still sobering to see it in black and white and have to admit that it is true. More than that, to have to realize that we are in one of those two groups, and then to search ourselves to make sure that we are hopefully not on the wrong side!

1. Do you know any Christians who are obviously running the race and fighting the fight? Are they the people who pray?

2. Why do you think prayer is the reason for this?
3. Why do you think the Holy Spirit loves to be begged?
4. Do you agree with this statement: "Prayer is the most definite cure against the devil and nagging sins"?

20

PRAYING IN THE POWER OF THE HOLY SPIRIT

"Not by might, nor by power, but by my Spirit, says the LORD of hosts"
Zechariah 4:6

When the Spirit really begins a work of conversion, He always carries that work to perfection. He brings about miraculous changes. He turns our character upside down. He causes old things to pass away, and all things to become new. The Holy Spirit is Almighty. With Him, nothing is impossible.

We never despair, because we believe in the power of the Holy Spirit. We can become depressed when we look at our own lives. We are often sick of ourselves. We might become depressed when we look at people in our congregations; they seem as hard and stubborn as a stone! But we remember the Holy Spirit, and what He has done. We remember the Holy Spirit and consider that He has not changed. He can come down like fire and melt the hardest hearts; He can convert the worst man or woman, and mold their whole character into a new shape. And so we hope, because of the Holy Spirit.

Our hearts need to understand that the growth of Christianity does not depend on human strength or power—but on the Lord's Spirit! We need to learn to lean less on pastors and to pray more for the Holy Spirit! We need to learn to expect less from schools, books, and church programs; and, while using all these methods diligently, to seek more passionately and sincerely for the outpouring of the Spirit!

Do you feel yourself being drawn toward God? Do you feel the smallest concern about your immortal soul? Does your conscience tell you that you have not yet felt the Spirit's power, and do you want to know what to do? Listen, and I will tell you. For one thing, you must go at once to Jesus in prayer, beg Him to have mercy on you and send you the Spirit. You must go directly to that open fountain of living waters, the Lord Jesus Christ, and you will receive the Holy Spirit (John 7:39). Begin at once to pray for the Holy Spirit. Do not think that you are closed and cut off from hope—the Holy Spirit is promised to those who ask Him. His name is the Spirit of Promise, and the Spirit of Life. Do not stop asking until He comes down and makes you a new heart. Cry out to the Lord—say to Him, "Bless me! Motivate and renew me, and make me alive!"

The Holy Spirit is always ready to help our weakness in prayer. It's one part of His role to assist us in our efforts to speak with God. We don't need to be depressed and worried with the fear of not knowing what to say, the Spirit will give us words if we just ask for His help. He will give us thoughts that breathe and words that burn. Our prayers as Christians are the inspiration of the Spirit—the work of the Holy Spirit who lives in us as the Spirit of grace and prayer. Surely we can hope to be heard. It's not us who are simply praying, but the Holy Spirit pleading in us. When we think about this, isn't this an encouragement?

The hand of the Spirit has not grown shorter! His power has not died out! He is like the Lord Jesus—the same yesterday, today, and forever. He is still doing miracles and will do so to the end. I will not be surprised to hear that the hardest man I know has become softened, and the proudest has come to bow down at the feet of Jesus as a child. I never become depressed about these things, because I believe in the power of the Holy Spirit.

Daily Reflection

The Holy Spirit is integral to prayer. After all, it is a spiritual duty, and He is the one that works, guides, and assists us in our prayers. But often, we miss out on His full capabilities in our lives—His power. We can only realize this through prayer —true, spiritual, heartfelt prayer.

1. Why does the Holy Spirit give us reason to hope?

2. Ryle spells out the way to feel the Spirit's power. What is it?
3. Why is the Spirit an encouragement in our praying?
4. Do you believe in the power of the Holy Spirit?

21

EVERYTHING WE NEED TO PRAY

"God is our refuge and strength, a very present help in trouble"
Psalm 46:1

P ower to help. Very few people in the world have that kind of power. Many want to do good for others—but they have no power. They have sympathy for others, and would relieve them if they could; they can cry with their friends in tough times but are unable to take their grief away. But even though people are weak, Jesus is strong. Even though our best friends are not able—Jesus is able and mighty! *"All authority in heaven and on earth has been given to me"* (Matt. 28:18). No one can do as much for us as a friend like Jesus. Others can be friends in the body—He can be a friend in body and soul. Others can do things for us for a short time—He can be a friend both for time and eternity!

God has everything necessary to make prayer easy if we will only give it a try. All things are ready on His side. Every objection we have, He has already anticipated. Every difficulty is provided for. The crooked places are made straight, and the rough places are made smooth. There is no excuse left for those of us who don't pray.

There is a way for every person, however sinful and unworthy they are, to draw near to God the Father. Jesus Christ has opened that way by the sacrifice He made for us on the cross. The holiness and justice of God shouldn't frighten sinners and keep them away. They just need to cry to God in the name of Jesus—plead the atoning blood of Jesus —and they will find God on a throne of grace, willing and ready to hear them. The name of Jesus is a passport for our prayers that never fails. In that name, we can come near to God with boldness and ask with confidence; God is ready to hear us. Isn't this an encouragement?

There is an advocate and intercessor that is always waiting to present the prayers of those who will let Him do so—Jesus Christ. He mixes our prayers with the incense of His almighty intercession so that they go up as a sweet fragrance before the throne of God. Poor as they are, they are mighty and powerful in the hand of our High Priest.

A check without a signature at the bottom is nothing but a worthless piece of paper. The stroke of a pen gives it all its value. The prayer of a poor child of Adam is weak on its own, but once endorsed by the hand of Jesus, it can achieve a lot. There was an officer in the city of Rome who was appointed to always have his doors open to receive any Roman citizen who applied to him for help. It is the same with the ear of Jesus, who is always open to the cry of everyone who wants mercy and grace. It's His role to help us. Our prayer is His delight. When you look at this, isn't this an encouragement?

Daily Reflection

We often think that prayer is our responsibility. While we have a major part to play, it is a conversation—a two-way correspondence. And as in every other facet of Christianity, God not only fulfills his end but ensures that everything we need is available, accessible, and free. It is humbling and encouraging to realize that He wants us to succeed.

1. Do you see God as wanting and able to help you? Or do you sometimes think He intentionally wants you to struggle and fail?
2. What has Jesus done to ensure we have access to God? Read Ephesians 2:18 and Hebrews 10:19.
3. What is Jesus' role as an advocate? Why do we need that?
4. What are your thoughts about the statement that your prayers are weak on their own?

22

THE DANGER OF NEGLECTING PRIVATE PRAYER

"But we are not of those who shrink back and are destroyed, but of those who have faith and preserve their souls"
Hebrews 10:39

There is such a thing as going backward in your faith after starting well once you've been born again. You might run well for a season, like the Galatians, and then turn away to false teachers. You might loudly claim your belief, while your feelings are warm, as Peter did; and then, in the hour of trial, deny your Lord. You may lose your first love, as the Ephesians did. You might cool down in your passion to do good, like Mark, the companion of Paul. You might follow an apostle for a season, and then, like Demas, go back to the world. All these things you could do. It's a miserable thing to be a backslider. Of all the terrible things that can happen to a person, I think this is the worst.

A stranded ship, a broken-winged eagle, a garden covered in weeds, a harp without strings, a church in ruins—all these are sad sights, but a backslider is still a much sadder sight. I don't doubt that true grace can ever be extinguished or a true relationship with Jesus can ever be broken off. But I do believe that a person might fall away so far that they can lose sight of their grace and question their salvation. And if this is not hell, it's certainly very close to it. A wounded conscience, a mind sick of itself, a memory full of self-criticism, a heart pierced through with the Lord's arrows, a spirit broken with a burden of accusation—this is all a taste of hell. It's hell on earth. The wise saying of Solomon is serious and worth noting, "*The backslider in heart will be filled with the fruit of his ways*" (Prov 14:14).

Now, what is the cause of most backsliding? I believe that one of the main causes is neglecting private prayer. Of course, the secret history of every person's fall from grace will not be known until the last day. I can only give my opinion as a minister of Christ, and a student of the heart. That opinion is, I repeat it clearly, that backsliding generally first begins with neglect of personal prayer.

Bibles read without prayer, sermons heard without prayer, marriages contracted without prayer, homes chosen without prayer, friendships formed without prayer, the daily act of private prayer itself rushed, or performed without heart—these are the downward steps that many Christians descend to a condition of spiritual paralysis, or they reach the point where God allows them to experience a significant fall.

This is the process that produces the lingering Lots, the unstable Samsons, the wife-idolizing Solomons, the inconsistent Asas, the pliable Jehosaphats, the over-careful Marthas—and there are so many of them to be found in the church. Often, the simple history of such cases is this: They became careless about personal prayer.

You can be very sure that people fall in private long before they fall in public. They are backsliders on their knees long before they backslide openly to the eyes of the world. Like Peter, they first ignore Jesus' warning to watch and pray; and then, like Peter, their strength is gone, and in the hour of temptation, they deny Him.

The world takes notice of their fall, and loudly mocks them, but doesn't know the real reason. Origen, the theologian and Father of the Faith in the early centuries after Jesus' death, ended up offering incense to an idol after being threatened by heathens with a punishment worse than death. Those nonbelievers boasted and gloated at his cowardice and denial of God, but they did not know the facts. Origen tells us in his writings that on that very morning he had left his room in a rush and did not finish his usual time of prayer.

If you are a true Christian, I trust you will never be a backslider. But if you don't wish to be a backsliding Christian, then pray.

Daily Reflection

Unfortunately, backsliding is a part of Christianity and has become common in our modern society. Most people start well but struggle to finish well. Somewhere along the way, despite our best intentions, we lose our way and our faith fades. Ryle is convinced that the reason is a lack of prayer!

1. Have you ever drawn back or slipped off in your Christian walk? What happened?
2. Do you agree that not praying is the reason for backsliding?
3. What do you think of Ryle's statement that, "people fall in private long before they fall in public"?
4. Read Luke 14:28-30 and compare it to what you have read in this chapter.

23

THE BEST RECIPE FOR JOY

*"You make known to me the path of life;
in your presence there is fullness of joy;
at your right hand are pleasures forevermore"*
Psalm 16:11

What is the best recipe for joy in a world like this? How can we get through this valley of tears with the least amount of pain? I don't know of any better recipe than the habit of taking everything to God in prayer.

This is the simple advice that the Bible gives, both in the Old and in the New Testament. What does the Psalmist say?

- *"Call upon me in the day of trouble; I will deliver you, and you shall glorify me"* (Psalm 50:15).

- "*Cast your burden on the LORD, and he will sustain you; he will never permit the righteous to be moved*" (Psalm 55:22).

What does Paul say?

- "*Do not be anxious about anything, but in everything by prayer and supplication with thanksgiving let your requests be made known to God. And the peace of God, which surpasses all understanding, will guard your hearts and your minds in Christ Jesus*" (Phil 4:6-7).

What does James say?

- "*Is anyone among you suffering? Let him pray*" (James 5:13).

This was the habit and custom of all the believers whose history is recorded in the Bible. This is what Jacob did when he feared his brother Esau. This is what Moses did when the people were ready to stone him in the wilderness. This is what Joshua did when Israel was defeated before Ai. This is what David did when he was in danger at Keilah. This is what Hezekiah did when he received the letter from Sennacherib. This is what the church did when Peter was put in prison. This is what Paul did when he was thrown into jail at Philippi.

Jesus Takes Our Sorrows

The only way to be joyful in a world like this is to always be casting all our cares on God. Trying to carry our burdens is what often makes us as Christians sad. If we only tell our troubles to God, He will help us to bear them as easily as Samson picked up and carried the gates of Gaza. If we decide to keep them to ourselves, then one day we will find that even a grasshopper is a burden.

There is a friend that is always waiting to help us if we will only offload our sorrow onto Him; a friend who had compassion for the poor, sick, and sorrowful, when He was on the earth; a friend who knows the heart of man, because He lived thirty-three years as a man amongst us; a friend who can cry with those who mourn, because He was a man of sorrows and knew grief very well; a friend who can help us, for there was no human pain that He could not cure. That friend is Jesus Christ.

The way to be joyful is to always open our hearts to Him. Oh, that we were all like that poor Christian slave; when he was threatened and punished, he just answered, "I must tell the Lord."

Jesus can make all those who trust Him and call on Him to be filled with joy, whatever their circumstances may be. He can give them peace of heart in a prison, contentment in poverty, comfort in times of grief, and joy when death is near. There is a mighty fullness in Him for all those who believe in Him—a fullness that is ready to be poured out on everyone who asks in prayer. If only people could understand that it does not depend on physical circumstances but on the state of the heart.

Prayer can make our cross lighter, no matter how heavy it is—it can bring One who will help us to bear them. Prayer can open a door for us when our way seems closed off—it can bring One who will say, "*This is the way, walk in it*" (Isaiah 30:21). Prayer can let in a ray of hope when all our earthly prospects seem dark—it can bring One who will say, "*I will never leave you nor forsake you*" (Heb. 13:5). Prayer can give relief to us when those we love most have died, and the world feels empty—it can bring One who can fill the gap in our hearts with Himself, and say to the waves within, "*Peace! Be still!*" (Mark 4:39). If only people were not so much like Hagar in the wilderness, blind to the well of living waters that are so near to them (Genesis 21:19).

Daily Reflection

Keep your Bible close during these reflections. In addition to Ryle referencing verses to substantiate what he is saying, you might think of other scriptures that relate. This is always good to extend and grow our understanding biblically. Write key verses down, and read them in other translations to make sure you grasp their meaning.

1. What do you think about Ryle's recipe for joy?
2. Do you agree with the words of the hymn:

"Oh, what peace we often forfeit

Oh, what needless pain we bear

All because we do not carry

Everything to God in prayer"

1. Have you ever experienced this as a result of prayer?

24

PRAYER IS NECESSARY FOR GROWTH

"Grow in the grace and knowledge of our Lord and Savior Jesus Christ"
2 Pet. 3:18

Do we grow in grace? Do we get on in our religion? Do we make progress?

WHEN I SPEAK of someone growing in grace, I mean their sense of sin is becoming deeper, their faith stronger, hope brighter, love more extensive, and spiritual-mindedness more marked. They feel more of the power of godliness in their heart and manifest more of it in their life. They are going from strength to strength, from faith to faith, and from grace to grace.

. . .

ONE THING essential to growth in grace is diligence in the use of private means of grace. This means private prayer, private reading of the Bible, and private meditation and self-examination. Someone who does not make any effort in these can never expect to grow. These are the roots of true Christianity. If you go wrong here, you will be wrong all the way through! This is the reason why many Christians never seem to get on. They are careless and lazy about their personal prayers. They only read their Bibles a little and with no sincerity. They have no time for self-inquiry and quiet thought about the state of their hearts.

In the church today, there is lots of activity, and many people "*run to and fro,*" hoping their "*knowledge shall increase*" (Dan. 12:4). Thousands are ready for public meetings, listening to sermons, or anything else that is a 'sensation.' Few appear to remember the necessity of making time to "*ponder in your own hearts on your beds, and be silent*" (Psalm 4:4). But without this, there is seldom any deep spiritual prosperity. Personal belief and faith must receive our first attention if we want our hearts to grow.

Regular and habitual communion with Jesus is essential to growth in grace. I am not referring to the Lord's Supper. I mean the daily habit of communion between the believer and his Savior, which is by faith, prayer, and meditation. You might be a believer and have your feet on the rock, but live far below your privileges. It is possible to have 'union' with Christ, and yet to have little if any 'communion' with Him.

The names and roles of Jesus show that this communion between Christians and their Savior is a real thing. Between the Bridegroom and His bride, between the Head and His members, between the Healer and His patients, between the Advocate and His clients, between the Shepherd and His sheep, between the Master and His students, there is a habit of familiar communion, of daily requesting for things needed, of daily pouring out and unburdening our hearts and minds. This habit is more than a vague general trust in the work that Jesus did for sinners. It is getting close to Him and taking hold of Him with confidence as a loving, personal Friend. This is communion.

No one will ever grow in grace if they do not know about the habit of communion. We must seek to have personal intimacy with the Lord Jesus and to deal with Him as a man deals with a loving friend. We must realize what it is to turn to Him first in every need, to talk to Him about every difficulty, to consult Him about every step, to spread before Him all our sorrows, to get Him to share in all our joys, to do all as in His sight, and to go through every day leaning on and looking to Him. This is the way that Paul lived: "*The life I now live in the flesh I live by faith in the Son of God*," "*To me to live is Christ*" (Gal. 2:20; Phil. 1:21). Living in this way, keeping constant communion with Christ—this is the person whose soul will grow.

Daily Reflection

We all want to grow—in knowledge, skill, and character—but do we see prayer as a stimulant that can produce the growth we want to see in our lives? As with most things, Ryle sees prayer as the key to growing and keeping our relationship intact.

1. Do you feel that you are growing in the Lord? Sometimes we need to ask others for a more accurate assessment.
2. Is your church full of activity but little prayer?
3. What is the connection between communion and growth?
4. Read John 15:4 and comment in regard to what you have read.

25

JESUS PRAYS FOR HIS PEOPLE

"I am praying for them. I am not praying for the world but for those whom you have given me, for they are yours"
John 17:9

Let us look at the verses that conclude the most wonderful prayer that was ever prayed on earth—Jesus' last prayer after the Last Supper. They contain three important requests that He offered up on behalf of His disciples.

To Sanctify Them

First, Jesus prays that His people may be sanctified. "*Sanctify them,*" He says, "*in the truth; your word is truth*" (John 17:17).

There is no doubt that the word 'sanctify' means "make holy." It is a prayer that the Father would make His people more holy, more spiritual, purer, and more saintly in thought, word, deed, life, and character. Grace had done something for the disciples already—called, converted, renewed, and changed them. Jesus prays that the work of grace may be carried higher and further and that His people may be more thoroughly sanctified and made holy in body, soul, and spirit—more like Himself.

Holy living trains Christians for heaven. The nearer we live to God while we live, the more ready we will be to dwell forever in His presence when we die. It is no wonder that increased sanctification should be the first thing that Jesus asks for His people.

To Unite Them

Secondly, we see how Jesus prays for the unity of His people. *"That they may all be one"*—as We are one—*"that the world may believe that you have sent me"* (John 17:21). This is an important request of His to the Father. There is no stronger proof of the value of unity among Christians, and the sinfulness of division, than the prominence which Jesus puts on it in His prayer.

Let this part of Jesus' prayer stay in our minds, and have a constant influence on our behavior as Christians. "*If possible, so far as it depends on you, live peaceably with all*" (Rom. 12:18). It was not for nothing that He prayed so fervently that His people might be "*one*."

To Be With Him

Finally, we see how Jesus prays that His people may, at last, be with Him and see His glory. "*I desire,*" He says, "*that they also, whom you have given me, may be with me where I am, to see my glory*" (John 17:24).

This is a beautiful and touching conclusion to Jesus' remarkable prayer. We might think it was meant to cheer up those who heard it and strengthen them for when He would leave them. But, this part of his prayer is full of incredible comfort.

In time, we will see Jesus face to face. We will be in His presence and company and never leave. If faith was wonderful, then seeing Him will be even better; and if hope has been sweet, certainty will be sweeter. No wonder Paul has written, "*we will always be with the Lord,*" and adds, "*Therefore encourage one another with these words*" (1 Thess. 4:17-18).

This wonderful prayer shows us three great requests. Let holiness and unity lead us, and Jesus' company be our result —do not let these out of our thoughts and minds.

Daily Reflection

It sometimes seems odd that Jesus had to pray since He was and is God. But in His obedience, and as an example to us, He prayed. It is interesting to observe what He prayed for, as this is also a template for our requests to God.

1. Do you ever pray that God will sanctify you?

2. Do you pray to be united with others and God in your Christian walk?
3. Do you pray to be with Jesus, now and for eternity?

26

SALVATION AND PRAYER

"For he says, 'In a favorable time I listened to you, and in a day of salvation I have helped you.' Behold, now is the favorable time; behold, now is the day of salvation"
2 Corinthians 6:2

I believe in salvation by grace as much as anyone else. I would gladly offer free and full forgiveness to the greatest sinner that ever lived, and stand by his death bed, and say, "Believe in the Lord Jesus, and you will be saved" (Acts 16:31). But I cannot see in the Bible that someone can have salvation without asking for it. For someone to receive forgiveness of his sins, but not lift up their heart, and say, "Lord Jesus, give it to me," I cannot find this anywhere. I can find evidence that no one can be saved by their prayers, but I can't find any that says you will be saved without prayer.

It is not absolutely necessary for salvation that you have to read the Bible. You might have no education, or be blind, and yet have Jesus in your heart. It is not absolutely necessary that you must publicly hear the preaching of the Gospel. He might live where the Gospel is not preached, or be confined to your bed, or deaf. But the same cannot be said about prayer. It is absolutely necessary for salvation that you pray.

In every journey, there must be a first step. There must be a change from sitting still to moving forward. The travels of Israel from Egypt to Canaan were long and tiring. Forty years passed before they crossed Jordan, yet there was someone who first moved when they marched from Ramah to Succoth. When does a person really take their first step in coming out from sin and the world? They do it on the day when they first pray with their heart.

In every building, the first stone must be laid, and the first blow must be struck. The ark took 120 years to build, but there was a day when Noah had to take his ax and start cutting the first tree down to form it. The temple of Solomon was a glorious building, but there was a day when the first huge stone was laid at the foot of Mount Moriah. When does the building of the Spirit really begin to appear in a person's heart? It begins when they first pour out their heart to God in prayer.

If you want salvation, and you want to know what to do, I advise you to go right now to Jesus Christ, in the first private place you can find, and beg Him in prayer to save your soul.

Tell Him that you've heard that He receives sinners, and has said, *"Whoever comes to me I will never cast out"* (John 6:37). Tell

Him that you are a poor and terrible sinner and that you come to Him on the faith of His invitation. Tell Him you put yourself completely into His hands—that you feel evil and helpless, and hopeless in yourself—and that unless He saves you, you have no hope at all to be saved. Beg Him to deliver you from the guilt, power, and consequences of sin. Beg Him to forgive you and wash you in His blood. Beg Him to give you a new heart, and put the Holy Spirit in your soul. Beg Him to give you grace, faith, will, and power to be His disciple and servant from this day forever. Go right now and tell these things to Jesus if you are sincere and true about your soul.

Tell Him in your own way, and in your own words. If a doctor came to see you when you're sick, you could tell him where you felt pain. If your heart feels the disease in it, surely you can find something to tell Christ.

Daily Reflection

Ryle's evangelical heart is evident here as he focuses on salvation and prayer. His sermons always had space for the lost to hear about God's saving grace. Here, he makes sure that we understand that we cannot simply be saved without calling out, asking for it, and confessing our need for God.

1. Do you agree that prayer is necessary for salvation?
2. Read Romans 10:13 and Acts 2:21 and comment.
3. Why do you think Ryle uses the words 'plead' and 'beg' so often when talking about this?
4. Can you recall your own salvation? What happened?

27

PRAYER IS YOUR RESPONSIBILITY

*"As I live, says the Lord, every knee shall bow to me,
and every tongue shall confess to God"*
Romans 14:11

The devil hates seeing us on our knees, yet I believe we should be suspicious of any prayers which cost us nothing. I believe we are very poor judges of the goodness of our prayers, and that the prayer which pleases us the least, often pleases God the most. Listen then, as a colleague in the Christian warfare, to offer you a few words of encouragement. At least we all feel that we must pray. We cannot give it up. We must go on.

No One Is Exempt

There is no easy, quick, royal path to health or learning. Princes and kings, poor men and workers, all have to attend to the needs of their bodies and minds. No one can eat, drink, or sleep by proxy or through someone else. No one can have another person learn the alphabet for them. All these are things that everybody must do for himself, or they will never be done.

Just as it is with the mind and body, so it is with the heart. There are certain things absolutely necessary for the heart's health and well-being. Each person has to look after these things for themselves. Each must repent for themselves. Each must come to Jesus for themselves. And each person must speak to God and pray. You must do it for yourself because nobody else can do it for you.

How can you expect to be saved by an 'unknown' God? And how can you know God without prayer? You know nothing of men and women in this world unless you speak to them. You cannot know God in Jesus unless you speak to Him in prayer. If you want to be with Him in heaven one day, you must be one of His friends on earth now. If you want to be one of His friends on earth, you must pray.

It Teaches Us

There will be many people at Jesus' right hand on the last day. All the saints gathered from north and south, and east and west will be a crowd that no one will be able to count. The song of victory that will come from their mouths, when their redemption is finally complete, will be a glorious song. It will be more than the noise of many rivers and mighty thunders, but there will be no one out of tune in that song, only harmony. They will sing with one heart and one voice; their experiences will be the same. All of them will have believed. All of them will have been washed in the blood of Jesus. All of them will have been born again. All of them will have prayed. Yes, we must pray on earth, or we will never praise in heaven.

We must go through the school of prayer, or we will never be ready for the time of praise.

To be prayerless is to be without God—without Jesus, without grace, without hope, and without heaven. It is as good as being on the road to hell. Now, can you understand why I ask the question—do you pray?

This is the point I want to bring you to—I want to know that you are praying. Your doctrinal views may be correct, and your love of the true Gospel may be unmistakable, but this could be nothing more than head knowledge and outward works. I want to know whether you know the throne of grace and whether you can speak to God as well as speak about God.

It is essential to your heart's health to make praying a part of every 24 hours in your life. Just as you give time to eating, sleeping, and business, so also give time to prayer. Choose your own hours and seasons. If nothing else, speak with God in the morning, before you speak with the world; and speak with God at night after you are finished with the world. But establish in your minds that prayer is one of the most important duties of every day. Don't push it into a corner. Don't give it the scraps and leftovers of your day. Whatever else you make a duty of, make a duty of prayer.

Daily Reflection

Although we read in chapter 21 that God does everything necessary for us to pray, we still have a responsibility. We still have to play our part in the two-way correspondence. Without this, we will find that our relationship will not grow.

1. Why does the devil hate seeing us on our knees? What does he do about it?
2. Read Matthew 7:21 in the light of the first part of this chapter. What do you understand by this?
3. Is it possible to know God without prayer?
4. What is the relationship between doing and knowing?

28

PRAYING FOR AN INCREASE OF FAITH

"The apostles said to the Lord, 'Increase our faith!'"
Luke 17:5

I encourage you, if you love life, and have found peace in believing, to pray daily for an increase of faith. Let your prayer always be, "Lord, increase my faith."

True faith has many degrees. The weakest faith is enough to secure salvation. A trembling hand may receive a healing medicine. The weakest baby may be heir to the richest possessions. The least faith gives a sinner a title to heaven, as much as the strongest faith—if it is true faith.

But "little faith" can never give as much comfort as strong faith. According to the degree of our faith will be the degree of our peace, hope, strength for duty, and patience in a trial. That is why we should always pray, "Increase our faith."

Do You Want More Faith?

Would you have more faith? Then make sure you are diligent—in your personal relationship with God—in watching your time, temper, and tongue—in your personal Bible-reading—in your personal prayers. It is useless to expect spiritual prosperity when we are careless about these things.

Would you have more faith? Then seek to become more acquainted with Jesus. Study Him as one who not only died for you, but is also living for you at the right hand of God—as one who not only shed His blood for you, but daily intercedes for you at the right hand of God—as one who is soon coming again for you, and will stand once more on this earth. The believer who is thoroughly acquainted with the fullness of Jesus grows from grace to glory. Then let your daily prayers always contain these words, "Lord, increase my faith."

Faith and Assurance

Faith is the root, and assurance is the flower. You can never have the flower without the root, but you can have the root and not the flower.

Faith is that poor woman who came behind Jesus and touched the hem of His garment (Mark 5:25). Assurance is Stephen standing calmly amid his murderers, and saying,

"Behold, I see the heavens opened, and the Son of Man standing at the right hand of God" (Acts 7:56).

Faith is the repentant thief crying, "*Jesus, remember me*" (Luke 23:42).

Assurance is Job sitting in the dust, covered with sores, and saying, "*For I know that my Redeemer lives*" (Job 19:25). "*Though he slay me, I will hope in him*" (Job 13:15).

Faith is Peter's drowning cry as he began to sink: "*Lord, save me*" (Matthew 14:30).

Assurance is Peter declaring before the Council, "*This Jesus is the stone that was rejected by you, the builders, which has become the cornerstone. And there is salvation in no one else, for there is no other name under heaven given among men by which we must be saved*" (Acts 4:11-12).

Faith is the anxious, trembling voice: "*I believe; help my unbelief!*" (Mark 9:24).

Assurance is the confident challenge: "*Who shall bring any charge against God's elect?... Who is to condemn?*" (Romans 8:33-34).

Faith is Saul praying in the house at Damascus, afraid, blind, and alone (Acts 9:11).

Assurance is Paul, the prisoner, looking calmly into the grave, and saying, "*I know whom I have believed*" (2 Tim. 1:12), "*there is laid up for me the crown*" (2 Tim. 4:8).

Faith is life. Assurance is more than life. It is health, strength, power, energy, activity, and beauty.

He who has faith does well. But he who has assurance does far better—sees more, feels more, knows more, enjoys more. You must begin with simple, child-like faith: "*Believe in the Lord Jesus, and you will be saved*" (Acts 16:31). But from faith go on to assurance where you can say, "*I know whom I have believed.*"

Make it your daily prayer that you may have an increase of faith. Cultivate that root and sooner or later you may have the flower. You may not attain full assurance at once—it is good sometimes to be kept waiting—wait for it. Seek and expect to find.

Daily Reflection

We often hear so much about faith that we almost take it for granted—much like prayer. It's either something we have a lot of or very little, depending on our state of heart. But here we read that we can have an increase of our faith and pray for more. Faith is synonymous with prayer. One without the other means very little. Assurance takes it to another level.

1. What does faith mean to you? Read Hebrews 11:1.
2. How does Ryle say that we can increase our faith in prayer?
3. How does assurance complete faith?
4. Read Hebrews 10:22. What do you understand about this verse having read this chapter?

29

RUSHED PRAYERS

"Be still before the LORD and wait patiently for him"
Psalm 37:7

I am convinced that prayer is just something that is thought to be a "matter of course," and like many matters of course, is badly neglected. It is "everybody's business," and so, is a business carried out by very few people. It's one of those private transactions between God and our souls that no one can see, and therefore there is the temptation to pass over and leave it undone.

No Real Prayer

I believe that thousands of people never say a word of prayer at all. They eat, drink, sleep, rise, go to work, and return to their homes. They breathe God's air, see His sun, walk on His earth, and enjoy His mercies. They have bodies that will die and have judgment and eternity before them, but they never speak to God. They live like the animals that die, behave like creatures without souls, and have nothing to say to Him who holds their life, breath, and all things, and from whose mouth they will one day receive their everlasting sentence. It is terrible, but also, unfortunately, very common!

I believe there are tens of thousands whose prayers are just a set of words repeated by rote, without a thought about their meaning. Some say a few quick sentences they picked up in the school when they were children. Some are content with repeating the words, forgetting that there is no real request in it. Some add the Lord's Prayer, but without the slightest desire that the serious things they ask for will be granted. Some who are homeless simply repeat the old lines: "Matthew, Mark, Luke, and John, bless the bed that I lie on."

No Heart in Prayer

Many, even those people who use the correct style and manner, mutter their prayers quickly after they have got into bed, or scramble over them while they wash or dress in the morning. They can think what they want, but in the sight of God, this is not praying. Words said without heart are as useless to our souls as the drum-beating of heathens before their idols. Where there is no heart, there may be lip service, but there is nothing that God listens to—there is no prayer. Saul, I have no doubt, said many long prayers before the Lord met him on the way to Damascus. But it was not until his heart was broken that God said, "*he is praying*" (Acts 9:11).

We probably won't ever be guilty of praying too much, but rather that Christians these days pray too little. On average, isn't the actual amount of time that many Christians give to prayer very small? These questions can't be answered satisfactorily, but I am afraid that most people's private devotions are very short and limited—just enough to prove they are alive, and no more. We seem to want and need very little from God. We have little to confess, little to ask for, and little to thank Him for. This is wrong.

Poor Prayers Are Not Answered

There is nothing more common than hearing believers complaining that they don't get on with each other. They tell us that they don't grow in grace, even though they want it. Isn't it actually true that many have as much grace as they ask for? Isn't it true that they have little because they ask little? The cause of their weakness is in their own stunted, clipped, contracted, hurried, little, narrow, small prayers. They have not, because they ask not.

We are not poor in Christ, but ourselves. Jesus says, "*Open your mouth wide, and I will fill it*" (Psalm 81:10). But we are like the king of Israel, who struck the ground three times and stopped when he was supposed to have struck it five or six times (2 Kings 13:18).

Daily Reflection

Every one of us is guilty of rushing our prayers at some time. We do it because we know we should pray but our hearts are not in it, and we have other more urgent things to attend to! We often rob ourselves because we listen to our emotions, our bodies, the circumstances, and our minds. The answer to real prayer is in the heart!

1. Have you ever rushed through or simply repeated your prayers? Why?
2. Why do you think we fall into the trap of giving lip service?
3. What is the significance of Paul having his heart 'broken'?
4. Do you agree with Ryle that poor or dead prayers are not answered?

30

ALERT, BOLD, AND SINCERE

"Let us therefore come boldly to the throne of grace, that we may obtain mercy and find grace to help in time of need"
Hebrews 4:16 NKJV

Alert in Prayer

We need to be alert in our prayers. Prayer is that point at which you must be on your guard. It is here that true religion begins—here it flourishes, and here it decays. Tell me what a man's prayers are, and I will be able to tell you the state of his heart. Prayer is the spiritual pulse; by this, spiritual health can always be tested. Prayer is the spiritual barometer; by this, we can always know if it is clear or cloudy in our hearts. Let us keep a close, continual eye on our private devotions.

Here is the core, marrow, and backbone of our practical Christianity. Sermons, books, tracts, committee meetings, and fellowship with good people are all good in their way, but they will never make up for the neglect of private prayer. Take a good look at the places, society, and companions that cause your hearts to drift away from communion with God, and make your prayers slow and ineffective. Be on your guard in those times. Observe the friends and duties that keep your heart in the right spiritual attitude, and when you are ready to speak with God, hold onto these and stay close. If you take care of your prayers, I can assure you that nothing will go very wrong with your heart.

Bold in Prayer

I want to emphasize the importance of boldness in prayer. There is a familiarity in some people's prayers which I don't like. But there is such a thing as a holy boldness, which should be desired.

- I am talking about the boldness like that of Moses when he pleaded with God not to destroy Israel; *"Why should the Egyptians speak, and say, 'He brought them out to harm them, to kill them in the mountains, and to consume them from the face of the earth'? Turn from Your fierce wrath, and relent from this harm to Your people"* (Exod 32:12).
- I am talking about the boldness like that of Joshua when the children of Israel were defeated before Ai: *"Then what will You do for Your great name?"* (Joshua 7:9).

- It's the same boldness for which Luther was remarkable. Someone heard him praying and said, "What a spirit, what a confidence was in his very expressions! With such a reverence he sued, as one begging of God, and yet with such hope and assurance, as if he spoke with a loving father or friend."
- This is the boldness that distinguished Bruce, a great Scot of the 17th century. His prayers were said to be "like bolts shot up into heaven."

Sadly, we also fall short in this area. We do not properly realize the privileges we have as believers. We do not plead as often as we should, "Lord, are we not Your people? Is it not for Your glory that we should be sanctified? Is it not for Your honor that the Gospel should increase?"

Sincere in Prayer

Another point is the importance of sincerity in prayer. It's not necessary for someone to have to shout, scream, or be very loud to prove that they are sincere. But we should be passionate, sincere, enthusiastic, and ask as if we were interested in what we were doing. It is the *"effective, fervent prayer"* that *"avails much,"* and not the cold, sleepy, lazy, lifeless one (James 5:16 NKJV). This is the lesson taught to us by the expressions used in the Bible about prayer. It's called "crying," "knocking," "wrestling," "laboring," and "striving."

This is the lesson taught to us by biblical examples.

- Jacob said to the angel at Penuel, "*I will not let You go unless You bless me!*" (Gen 32:26).
- Daniel pleaded with God, "*O Lord, hear! O Lord, forgive! O Lord, listen and act! Do not delay for Your own sake, my God*" (Daniel 9:19).
- It was written about Jesus, "*In the days of His flesh, when He had offered up prayers and supplications, with vehement cries and tears*" (Heb. 5:7).

How different these are to many of our own prayers that seem tame and lukewarm in comparison! I am sure God would say to many of us, "You do not really want what you pray for!"

Daily Reflection

This chapter speaks about being engaged! If we are not alert, bold, or sincere, we will be lacking in the prayers we bring to God in one way or another. By engaging our minds and hearts, we can truly speak with Him, and He will answer.

1. How can we be alert in prayer?
2. What is the difference between being bold and arrogant?
3. What do you think it means to be sincere in prayer?

31

MISSIONARY PRAYER

"The harvest is plentiful, but the laborers are few; therefore pray earnestly to the Lord of the harvest to send out laborers into his harvest"
Matthew 9:37-38

Do we want to help see Christianity grow in the world? Then let us never forget to pray for ministers, especially for young men about to enter the ministry.

Prayer is one of the best and most powerful methods of helping forward the cause of Christ in the world. It is within reach of all who have the Spirit of adoption. Not all believers have money to give to missions. Very few have great intellectual gifts or extensive influence among people. But all believers can pray for the success of the Gospel, and they should pray for it every day. Many incredible answers to prayer are recorded in the Bible. *"The prayer of a righteous person has great power as it is working"* (James 5:16).

More prayer is needed among us. I am not saying there is no prayer for the success of missions, but I am saying there is far too little. We do not seem to realize the importance of prayer or believe its power. We moan about the lack of success, but do we use the proper means to obtain it? We want to see more ministry in reaching the lost, but do we go the right way to bring it about? Aren't we neglecting the strongest tool of success within our reach? Wouldn't God say to us, "You have little because you ask little... Open your mouths wide and they shall be filled!"

We want the right sort of missionaries and are often sad because there seem to be so few. But we forget that it is not money and colleges but the Holy Spirit alone who can make a person ready to become a missionary. We have the command, *"The harvest is plentiful, but the laborers are few; therefore pray earnestly to the Lord of the harvest to send out laborers into his harvest"* (Matt. 9:37-38). Prayer is the strongest engine that we can use. It is better than money. Like the dew in summer, it makes no noise, it is unseen—but it produces incredible results. It requires no learning except the teaching of the Spirit. It requires no books and expensive machinery to keep it going. The old, the blind, the sick, the crippled—all can pray and obtain mighty blessings if they will. Yet prayer is the last engine that we generally resort to, and the most difficult to persuade people to continue using.

We often hear the words at the end of a sermon: "I am sure you will pray." I wish it was practiced as often as it is preached.

If we want to help the cause of missions, we must pray more. The Lord's arm has not grown shorter since the days of the Bible. The Spirit is still mighty to pull down strongholds. The outpouring of the Spirit is needed and must be sought.

Never were there so many open doors of usefulness, so many fields white to the harvest. Use those open doors, and help to reap those fields.

Make sure that by God's help you will leave the world a better world when you leave it. Remember the souls of relatives, friends, and companions. The time is short, the sand is running out of the glass of this old world; redeem the time. Whether you see the fruits of your prayer in others or not, you can be sure that your efforts will always do good for yourself. *"One who waters will himself be watered"* (Prov. 11:25).

Daily Reflection

Praying for others is important, as we often get into a habit of only bringing ourselves before the Lord. The Bible is full of examples of people praying for others or asking for prayer. When our hearts are expanded to include requests for others and reaching the lost, we begin praying powerful prayers.

1. Do you ever pray specifically for those reaching out to the unsaved people?

2. Do you have a heart for the lost?
3. How do people become missionaries?
4. Ryle says that we will see fruits in our own lives if we pray like this. What does he mean?

ABOUT J.C. RYLE

John Charles Ryle was born in England on 10 May 1816 into an upper-class family. He achieved great results in his education and sports during his schooling years, especially in cricket and rowing. But a serious chest infection brought all of it to a halt just before his final exams.

His sickness and being bed-ridden drew him back to the Bible, and in 1837, during a church service, he was born again after hearing a reading from Ephesians chapter 2.

Any chance of further studies and entering politics ended as a result of his recurring infection and the untimely closure of his father's bank. Instead, he trained in the Church of England, becoming an ordained minister in 1841.

He was a minister in a few local parishes, where he married his first wife; however, she became sick and died shortly after. He then remarried to his second wife, who also later passed away. Finally, he became the vicar of All Saints in Suffolk in 1861. It was here that he became known for his direct approach to preaching and firm stand on the church's role and relevance as an evangelical light to the world. Several books were written and published covering many different topics, from prayer and the church to the Gospel of John.

In 1880, Ryle was appointed as the first Anglican Bishop of Liverpool under Prime Minister Benjamin Disraeli's advice. In line with his evangelical calling, he began to focus his energies on building churches and mission halls to reach out to the urban areas around the city.

At the age of 83, after losing his third wife, he retired and later died that same year, in 1900.

BIBLIOGRAPHY

Crossway. (2001). *English Standard Version Bible*. Crossway Bibles.

Grace Gems! (n.d.). www.gracegems.org. Retrieved May 20, 2022, from https://www.gracegems.org/

Holman Bible Publishers. (2016). *The Holy Bible: NKJV New King James Version*. - Holman Bible Publishers.

www.ingramcontent.com/pod-product-compliance
Lightning Source LLC
LaVergne TN
LVHW020441070526
838199LV00063B/4812